Straight Talk
About
Teenage Suicide

Straight Talk About Teenage Suicide

Bernard Frankel, Ph.D., and Rachel Kranz

☑® Facts On File, Inc.

Straight Talk About Teenage Suicide

Facts On File, Inc.
11 Penn Plaza
New York NY 10001

Library of Congress Cataloging-in-Publication Data
Frankel, Bernard.
    Straight talk about teenage suicide/Bernard Frankel and Rachel Kranz.
        p. cm.
    Includes index.
    ISBN 0-8160-3751-5 (pbk)
    1. Teenagers—United States—Suicidal behavior—Juvenile
literature. 2. Suicide—United States—Prevention—Juvenile
literature. [1. Suicide.] I. Kranz, Rachel. II. Title.
HV6546.F75 1994
362.2′8′083—dc20   93-38381

Facts On File books are available at special discounts when purchased in bulk quantities for businesses, associations, institutions or sales promotions. Please call our Special Sales Department in New York at 212/967-8800 or 800/322-8755.

You can find Facts On File on the World Wide Web at
http://www.factsonfile.com

Cover design by Smart Graphics
Printed in the United States of America

MP FOF 10 9 8 7 6 5 4 3 2 1

This book is printed on acid-free paper.

Contents

Special thanks to Erin.

1

A Rising
Epidemic

Maria* is known around school as a tough kid. Nothing gets to her—no one scares her and nothing seems to bother her. She has kind of a wild reputation, drinking a lot at parties on weekends and doing all different kinds of drugs. Some of the kids think she even carries a knife, and a lot of people are scared of her, believing that she'll cut them if they get on her bad side. It's easy to get on Maria's bad side—she has a sharp temper, and she's quick to respond with an insult or a shove if you get in her way.

What no one knows about Maria is that she carries a razor blade around in her wallet. If something bothers her, she takes out the blade and scratches herself with it, on the arms or the legs. Bleeding a little makes her feel better, as if the bad feelings are bleeding out of her. So far she hasn't hurt herself too badly. But whenever she has a really bad day,

---

* All of the stories of teenagers in this book are based on *composites*—fictional portraits of teenagers that make use of the real elements of teenagers' lives.

she thinks about her razor blade—her safety net. She thinks about how she could kill herself, and then she would never have a bad day again.

Charles seems to have it made. He's a straight-A student, a football star, and president of the student council. His girlfriend is one of the cutest girls in school, and he has a whole crowd of people that he hangs out with. His parents seem to be the coolest parents you can imagine. They give him a good allowance, bought him a car for his 16th birthday, are relaxed about curfews and chores, and enjoy joking and laughing with Charles and his two younger sisters.

Although most courses come easily to Charles, he is having a hard time with chemistry. Even though he's studied harder for this class than for any other he's ever taken, he just can't seem to get it. He's been getting B minuses and C pluses on his tests and projects—a respectable average for most students, but Charles expects more from himself. How will he ever get to the top college he's been planning for if he doesn't have the top grades in his class? One day Charles takes a chemistry midterm and he just panics. He's so anxious about the test that he can't think at all. When the test papers come back, he discovers just how badly he did—a D. Charles has never gotten a D in his life, and he's devastated. He can't imagine what his parents will say, or the school guidance counselor, or the admissions committee at the colleges he's applying to. He can't stand the thought of facing them. He thinks, "It would be easier to kill myself than to face them like this."

Evie has always been kind of a loner, but since she's gotten to high school, she's spent even more time by herself. Her father died when she was 10, and eventually her mother had to sell the house where Evie had grown up and move to another city, where she could get a better job. The few friends Evie had from elementary school live so far away that she never sees them anymore; her father's brother, her favorite uncle, moved to yet another city. Sometimes Evie feels like her life is divided into two parts, her old town and her new town—and neither one is quite like home.

Evie likes to read all kinds of books, and she likes to write poetry. She's not much interested in clothes and makeup, and sometimes it seems like all the girls in her new town only want to go the mall, which she finds boring. The other kids think Evie is kind of strange, and they often tease her about the plain way she dresses and the "weird" things she likes to do. Usually Evie just ignores them, but there are days when it really gets to her. She's starting to feel like she'll never have any friends and no one will ever really care about her. She finds herself imagining what it would be like if she died. She pictures herself lying in her coffin, really peaceful and looking beautiful. Then she thinks of who would be at her funeral. Her uncle would come in from his faraway city, her busy mother would take time off from work, and all the kids at school would be there too. Evie thinks that if she died, *then* everyone would be sorry that they didn't appreciate her more.

The Mystery of Suicide

Statistics show that virtually everyone reading this book is likely to know someone who has committed suicide, attempted suicide, or seriously considered suicide at some point in his or her life. The decision to kill oneself is a painful and profound choice, affecting not only the person who making the decision but also all who know and love that person.

Perhaps the most agonizing aspect of suicide is its difficulty to understand. It leaves hundreds of questions and no answers. The answers can come only from the one who died, and he or she is not available. We might realize that a suicidal person was depressed, angry, unhappy, or scarred; feeling hopeless, lonely, guilty, or at wit's end. We might understand the various factors that helped make the decision seem possible or even necessary: drugs and alcohol; an unwanted pregnancy; abuse from parents or other adults; fears about grades; the loss of a loved one through death, rejection, divorce, or a recent move. We might look at social factors or personal ones, political issues or pyschological theories, immediate life events or a person's entire history. Yet for every explanation we might find, we could find another person in the same condition who did *not* commit suicide. What pushed the actual suicide over the edge? What made the difference between choosing life and choosing death?

Writers, philosophers, and those who survive after a beloved person's suicide have sought these answers for many centuries. Sometimes a suicide might even seem to "make sense"—for example, the person had a fatal disease that caused great pain, or was heading into an old age of poverty and senility, or was condemned to a lifetime in prison under horrible conditions. But what explains the self-imposed death of a young person, a teenager who has an entire lifetime to look forward to?

In a sense, there are no answers to these questions. No one can explain such a weighty and final decision but the person who makes it. Why a particular person commits or attempts suicide may remain a mystery, unless the person survives the attempt and has the chance to find a deeper understanding afterward.

What we can do, however, is to understand in a more general way how and why people might come to see suicide as an answer to their problems. We can look for the ways of thinking and feeling that seem to lead to this ending, in the hopes of opening up other options, other choices. We can search for a deeper understanding of the elements in our world that might drive a person to suicide, with an eye toward deciding what we'd like to change in the world around us. And we can learn to recognize the warning signs of suicide, so that we can get help for ourselves or reach out to our friends.

In this chapter, we'll begin with an overview: a statistical picture of teenage suicide and a quick look at the myths and facts about this difficult problem. In Chapter 2, we'll go on to look at how people come to this decision, discovering that many people decide to commit suicide as the result of a loss, a disappointment, or a feeling of depression. In Chapter 3, we'll look at why some people may have a more difficult time withstanding these events, so that a loss that one person finds merely painful another person experiences as simply unbearable. In Chapter 4, we'll discuss how suicidal people might get help, breaking out of the isolation and hopelessness that made death seem like the only solution. In Chapter 5, we'll look at suicide from the point of view of friends and family: how to recognize that someone may be considering suicide, how to reach out to someone who is, and how to survive the loss of someone who has already made that decision. Finally, in Chapter 6, we'll provide some resources for anyone who is concerned about suicide, depression, or any other personal problem that might seem overwhelming.

A Growing Problem

Suicide is the third most frequent cause of death among teenagers—after accidents and homicide.* Traditionally, young people have had a very low rate of suicide: Suicide rates tend to go up with age and to really take off among people over 60. Even today, people between the ages of 15 and 24 have the lowest suicide rate of any adult age group.

Nevertheless, teenage suicide has become an increasingly painful problem because the rate of teenage suicide has tripled over the last 40 years. An increasing number of young people are ending their own lives; many others make suicide

---

* Except where cited, all statistics in this chapter are from *The Enigma of Suicide* by George Howe Colt, 1991.

attempts without actually dying; still more, like Maria, Charles, and Evie, consider suicide.

Statistics on suicide can be misleading since, without a note, it is often difficult to distinguish suicides from accidents. In addition, because of the stigma that often surrounds suicide in our society, many official reports will cover up suicides by reporting them as accidents. For example, if a young person is found dead with a gun in his or her hand, a doctor or medical examiner may well call the death accidental, rather than considering the possibility that the shooting was intentional. Still further confusion arises from the fact that many young people engage in risky behavior—such as reckless driving, violent fighting, or foolhardy acts under the influence of drugs or alcohol—that puts them in the path of death. Many experts believe that this type of behavior, carrying as it does the possibility of dying, is actually a form of suicidal behavior. Thus the major cause of teenage death—accidents—may also include a great number of suicides.

Tragically, although the mortality rate (the percentage of deaths within a given population) has gone down for every other age group over the past 30 years, it has actually gone up for those between 15 and 24—because of the increase in suicide. Since 1950, the suicide rate has increased by 300 percent for those between the ages of 10 and 14. (Health statisticians do not recognize suicide in children younger than 10, although some psychologists believe that, in fact, children as young as three have attempted and even completed suicides.)

Suicide actually is even more pressing for those just past teen age. It is the second leading cause of death for those between the ages of 20 and 24. Again, although accidents are the major cause of death for this age group, many accidents may be attributed to suicide or suicidal behavior. Compared to 15- to 19-year-olds, twice as many 20- to 24-year-olds kill themselves.

People who gather statistics lump these two age groups together and consider those from age 15 to age 24 as one group. In 1950, only 4.5 people per 100,000 in this age group killed themselves. By 1977, this figured had tripled, to 13.6 people.

In the 1980s, the figures continued to rise. According to a 1993 report from the Centers for Disease Control and Prevention, the teen suicide rate rose between 1979 and 1988, with suicide responsible for 12 percent of the deaths among people between the ages of 10 and 24. According to the same report, the number of suicides among people 10 to 14 years old rose from 151 in 1979 to 237 in 1988, an increase of 75 percent. Among people between 15 and 19, the number increased from 1,788 suicides in 1979 to 2,870 in 1988, an increase of 34.5 percent.

Similar figures were reported in the May 25, 1993 edition of the *Wall Street Journal*. A survey conducted by Northwestern National Life Insurance found that teen suicide rates had increased in 37 of the 50 states during the 1980s (although the rates did fall in 12 states and remained unchanged in one state). Nationwide, however, the teen suicide rate increased 18 percent during the 1980s. According to the *Wall Street Journal's* description of the report, "the teen suicide rise stems largely from higher levels of teen stress, drug and alcohol abuse, and unresolved family conflicts."

The teen suicide rate continued to stay high in the 1990s. In 1990, according to a Centers for Disease Control study published in the October 5, 1991 *Science News*, one in 12 U.S. high school students attempted suicide. In 1991, according to a September 1993 report prepared by John L. McIntosh for the American Association of Suicidology, 4,751 young people between the ages of 15 and 24 killed themselves, a rate of 13.1 percent per 100,000 people in that age range.

And, in all likelihood, the real suicide rate is two to three times higher than the official rate, for all the reasons we've described.

For every teenager who actually commits suicide, many more seriously consider it or make some kind of attempt, putting them at risk for future possible completed suicides.

A poll conducted for Empire Blue Cross and Blue Shield by the Gallup organization and published in the April 4, 1993 issue of the *New York Times* reported that 6 percent of American teenagers reported a suicide attempt, with 15 percent saying that they had come "very close to trying." A Centers for Disease Control study reported in the May 1992 *Phi Delta Kappan* presented an even grimmer picture: 27 percent of the high school students surveyed said that they had "thought seriously" about committing suicide in the previous year, while 8 percent-one in 12—said they had actually made a suicide attempt.

Although black Americans have a lower suicide rate than white Americans, over the past few decades their suicide rate has also increased. In the 25 years between 1966 and 1991, suicide among young black American men more than doubled.

According to an article in the October 27, 1989 issue of the *Journal of the American Medical Association*, suicide rates among black men are highest for the 25- to 34-year age group; nevertheless, observers are also concerned about the suicide rate for black male teenagers. Interestingly, although the rate of black male suicides was 12.1 percent in 1991, according to the American Association of Suicidology report of September 1993, the rate for black women was only 1.9 percent. (No data are available breaking these figures down by age, but we may assume that there is a similar gap between male and female suicide rates among black teenagers.)

Native Americans have the highest teenage suicide rate of any ethnic group in the United States. According to the National Center for Health Statistics, in 1990, some 252 Native Americans committed suicide (214 men, 38 women). Surveys of American Indian youth found their suicide rates shockingly high as well. A survey of 13,454 seventh- through 12th-grade American Indian-Alaska Native youths who attended high school in eight nonurban areas from across the country revealed that almost 6 percent of the students surveyed revealed signs of "severe emotional distress," while 16.9 percent had actually attempted suicide. Results of this study were published in the March 25, 1992 edition of the *Journal of the American Medical Association.* However, the shocking increase in the overall U.S. 15- to-24-year-old suicide rate comes from the dramatic increase in suicides committed by white people—specifically, white men—between the ages of 20 to 24. According to Kim Smith, of the Menninger Foundation, an organization that sponsors research on mental health, five times as many young males as females actually commit suicide, although three times as many young females attempt it.

Smith also provides a disturbing picture of the extent of teenage suicide. She says that some 2 percent of all high school students have made at least one suicide attempt, accounting for some 2 million high school students. Another study, cited by George Howe Colt in *The Enigma of Suicide,* reports that at least 50 percent of the teenagers questioned had "seriously considered" suicide at least once before they graduated. Some 20 percent of those questioned said that they were "empty, confused, and would rather die than live." At least 58 percent had known someone who had attempted suicide; 10 percent had tried it themselves.

These figures are confirmed by Los Angeles psychiatrist Michael Peck who, was quoted by Colt in 1991 as concluding that up to 10 percent of the young people in any high school are at some risk. Another statistic cited by Colt holds that for every adult suicide, there are approximately 10 adults who attempt to kill themselves without actually doing so; however, for teenagers, every completed suicide indicates 20 or more suicide attempts. The figures add up to an overall rate of some 1 to 2 percent of Americans in all age groups who die by suicide, with approximately 4 to 5 percent of all Americans making some kind of suicide attempt.

What should we make of these disturbing statistics? Although the vast majority of young people do not commit or even attempt suicide, a sizable number of young people do.

Furthermore, all young people are affected by a climate in which many people whom they know may consider taking their own lives—and in which at least one person whom they know may actually do so.

Does suicide grow by example? Are people more likely to kill themselves if they know others who have done so—or if they listen to songs about suicide? Watch made-for-television movies on the topic? Read or watch major news stories about other teenagers who took their own lives?

The widespread publicity given to "cluster" suicides has both awakened public consciousness about teen suicide and given rise to many myths about how the decision to kill oneself actually is reached. Let us examine the distressing phenomenon of "cluster" suicides, as well as the question of how publicity and public discussion might affect people's decisions.

Suicide by Example

Although it was the so-called cluster suicides in the late 1970s and early 1980s that first brought teenage suicide into the national consciousness, experts do not agree on whether "clusters" actually exist. How does one person's decision to commit suicide affect another person's decision? And, perhaps more important, how does the publicity surrounding a suicide affect other people's decisions? What kind of impact do rock music, made-for-TV movies, and similar cultural expressions have on young people's willingness to live or die?

These are not new questions. As far back as 1774, when the German author Johann Wolfgang von Goethe published *The Sorrows of Young Werther*, young people seemed attracted to suicidal "role models." In Goethe's famous novel, young Werther kills himself when he cannot have the woman of his dreams. This famous book, a classic of German literature, published by one of the world's greatest authors, was blamed for the phenomenon known as

Wertherism, in which hundreds of young men chose romantic suicides like the one Goethe described. Even at the time, people debated whether Goethe's work was responsible for inspiring suicide, or whether it was merely reflecting the mood of the time.

A similar question arose more recently, when rock musicians like Ozzy Osbourne were accused of inspiring suicide in their teenage listeners. Once again, critics argued that the rock songs put compelling ideas into the heads of impressionable young adolescents, while defenders claimed that no one commits suicide because of a song.

Sociologists have debated this question as well. Sociologist David Phillips compared vital statistics to the *New York Times* index to find out what effect highly publicized stories about suicide had on actual self-imposed deaths. He found that the number of suicides increased significantly after each big suicide story. After the story's effect wore off, usually about a month later, the suicide rate returned to normal—but it never went *lower* than it had been previously. Thus, Phillips concluded, the suicides that followed the stories were "extra" suicides, rather than ones that would have occurred sooner or later anyway. After the suicide of movie star Marilyn Monroe in 1962, for example, the suicide rate jumped up by 12 percent—197 more suicides were committed in the month after her death.

Those who agree with Phillips's work use the analogy of an advertisement. If you are watching television, they claim, and you experience some vague feeling, you might see an ad for a fast-food restaurant. The ad helps you to understand that vague feeling as hunger and to think of satisfying the hunger by going to a restaurant, perhaps even the one described in the ad. Likewise, they explain, people with a vague feeling of unhappiness might decide from the story of another's suicide that suicide is also a solution for them.

Phillips went on to publish a well-known study of response to other suicides in the *New England Journal of Medicine* in 1986. He and his colleagues examined the effect of 38 nationally televised news or feature stories about suicide broadcast during the years 1973 to 1979. They found an average 7 percent increase in teenage suicides during the week after each story, although adult suicides did not increase at all. The more networks that ran the story, the bigger the increase in teen suicide. According to Phillips and his colleagues, girls were more susceptible to suggestion than boys.

Madelyn Gould and David Shaffer, working out of Columbia University, published a similar study in the same journal, also in 1986. Studying four made-for-TV movies aired during a six-month period from 1984 to early 1985, they found that teenage suicide in the metropolitan New York area rose in the two weeks after broadcast of three of the four movies. According to their study, six more teenagers than would otherwise have been expected to, committed suicide. Suicide attempts, they found, rose by 40 percent.

As might be expected, the television networks themselves denied any link between their broadcasts and the increase in young people killing themselves. Sociologists employed by NBC to study the data found no overall increase in the suicide rate for 1984, although they did find an increase during the years 1977 to 1980. In other words, while teenage suicide had been going up a few years earlier, there was no evidence that its rise had been inspired by the television broadcasts. The slight increase in teen suicide that the researchers had noted when they looked at a two-week period was not visible when the year as a whole was examined; this fact suggests that the increase was either a coincidence or reflected suicides that might have been committed anyway, sooner or later.

Phillips himself went on to contradict Gould and Shaffer in a 1987 study in which he looked at the effect of those same made-for-TV movies on teens in California and Pennsylvania. According to his research, the television broadcasts had no effect at all. Psychologist Alan Berman also looked at the TV movies' effect, studying the statistics from 19 medical examiners across the country, representing 20 percent of the U.S. population. In his study, there was no increase in teen suicides during the two weeks after the television broadcasts; in fact, in some areas, there were even decreases. However, he did believe that the broadcasts may have influenced the *methods* of suicide chosen by young people who were already determined to kill themselves during the same period.

Cluster Suicides

Even if TV movies and newspaper articles don't affect a teenager's decision to commit suicide, do more immediate examples have an effect? If a young person knows of one or several people in the community who have chosen suicide as a "solution" to their problems, is that young person more likely to choose suicide as well?

These questions were raised dramatically in the late 1970s and early 1980s, when "clusters" of teenage suicides began to appear: that is, several suicides within the same community took place in a relatively short time. Consider the following examples of cluster suicides:

- 1974, San Mateo County, California: 11 teen suicides in bedroom communities near San Francisco.
- 1978, Chappaqua, Westchester County, New York: 2 suicides in the local high school in three months; 5 suicide attempts in 7 weeks.
- 1978, Chicago's North Shore: the beginning of a 17-month period that saw 28 teen suicides, earning the region the nickname of "the Suicide Belt."
- 1979, West Milford, New Jersey: the beginning of a 20-month period that saw 6 teen suicides.
- 1980, Englewood, Colorado: 3 suicides in 5 months, all at the same high school.

- 1982, Cheyenne, Wyoming: 3 teen suicides in 17 days.
- 1983, Columbus, Ohio: 5 teen suicides in one month, with three freshmen at the same high school committing suicide over the same weekend.
- 1983, Plano, Texas: the beginning of a 14-month period that saw 8 teen suicides in this wealthy Dallas suburb.
- 1984, Beverly Hills, California: 3 teen suicides between January and April.
- 1984, Arlington, Texas: 5 teen suicides in 4 months in this well-off Dallas suburb.
- 1984, Westchester area, New York: 8 teen suicides in 4 months.
- 1987, Bergenfield, New Jersey: two sisters and two young men killed themselves on a suicide pact.
- 1987, a Chicago suburb: two young women committed suicide only a few days after the Bergenfield deaths.
- 1992, Sheridan, Arkansas: four high school student suicides in a single month.

At first glance, these statistics seem impressive evidence that clusters do in fact exist. Other data and studies would also seem to support the thesis that one suicide can set off others, provoking an "epidemic" of suicide as the "germ" spreads. Psychologists and sociologists have long noticed, for example, that confined places or closed societies often experience suicides in closely spaced series. Army barracks, boarding schools, colleges, mental hospitals, and prisons have all been prey to groups of "clusters" of suicides, in which one death seems to inspire others. Observers believe that adolescents are especially prone to "suicide by imitation," since they are particularly vulnerable to peer pressure and to imitating others in their quests for their own identities. As Westchester psychiatrist Samuel Klagsburn says, "When one kid actually goes ahead and does the unthinkable, it's almost as if it gives permission to others to also do the unthinkable."

Another version of "suicide by imitation" is the case where young people actively agree together to commit suicide, the so-called suicide pact. The March 26, 1990 issue of *Macleans* reported on the suicides of three 14-year-old boys in the town of Lethbridge, Alberta, Canada. All three boys died between December 15, 1989 and March 8, 1990 in what some police officers believed may have been a suicide pact. According to *Macleans,* "more than 50 of [Lethbridge's] boys and girls may have been involved in planned suicide pacts."

Likewise, a *New York Times* article of January 24, 1992 reported on two youths from Greenwich, Connecticut who had apparently agreed to end their lives together in a park near the prosperous suburban town.

Yale researchers Bruce Rounsaville and Myra Weissman conducted a study, published in 1980, that seemed to bear out the idea that young people's decisions to kill themselves could be influenced by others examples. In their examination of 62 patients in emergency care after an attempted suicide, Rounsaville and Weissman found that four had made their attempts within four weeks of the suicide or suicide attempt of someone they were close to. In three out of the four cases, they used a similar method to that used by the person who made the previous suicide attempt.

Yet even if this study is valid, it still accounts for only four out of 62 attempted suicides, or about 6 percent. And according to the Centers for Disease Control, "cluster" suicides account for no more than about 5 percent of all teenage suicide.

"Reading about a suicide does not *make* someone suicidal," says Judie Smith, program director at the Suicide and Crisis Center in Dallas. Smith worked with members of the Plano, Texas community after the local "cluster" of 1983. She agrees that no one who is not already seriously considering suicide will be affected by reports of others' deaths. However, she cautions, "if that person is already at risk of suicide, the media reports may inadvertently convey the message that it's okay to kill yourself, that suicide is an acceptable solution to your problems." This message may be reinforced by a community's reaction to a teen suicide, in which, say, a previously ignored student is suddenly given attention, even praise—after he or she is dead.

The question still remains whether the "cluster" suicides reflected a copycat effect, a statistical accident, or a common response to a common set of problems. For example, Smith's community of Plano may have nurtured a set of conditions that were particularly conducive to suicide. The area had grown quite rapidly, from 17,000 in 1970 to 90,000 in 1983, a growth consisting mainly of affluent professionals whose income was 50 percent higher than the national norm. Many of Plano's residents had been recently separated from family and community, creating an atmosphere of rootlessness and alienation in which teenagers might easily feel cut off and isolated. These conditions of isolation—and not a copycat effect per se—may have been responsible for Plano's unusually high suicide rate in 1983 and early 1984.

The so-called Westchester cluster of 1984, on the other hand, may have been more of a statistical accident than anything else. The press may have inadvertently linked a number of unrelated suicides, following the notion of the "suicide cluster." Many of the Westchester suicides came from affluent families—but many others came from poor or middle-income families. In fact, the eight suicides in four months that constituted the famous "cluster" actually took place in three separate counties, and many of the young people involved had never met or heard of one another. If just Westchester County alone was considered, apart from its neighbors, only six teenage suicides occurred in 1984, compared with an average of five over the eight years before—and compared with the previous high of seven teen suicides in 1979. In that case, the suicide rate of 1984 hardly counts as an "epidemic" for Westchester County, despite the way the press chose to report the story.

Many experts believe that "cluster" suicides are more a function of the rise and fall of interest in the press than of actual statistical trends. According to the Centers for Disease Control, there has never been a scientifically standard way to track suicide clusters among teenagers. That is, there is no uniform definition of "cluster" that can be used to determine whether a suicide is part of a cluster or stands as its own isolated event.

An article in the November 25, 1989 issue of *Science News* reported on a study by psychiatrist Lucy E. Davidson that throws further doubt on the concept of clusters. While working for the Centers for Disease Control, Davidson studied the two Texas suicide "clusters" of 1983 and 1984. According to the article, she found "no evidence that people not already at risk of suicide are more likely to take their own lives after exposure to other suicides."

In any case, as we have seen, the best estimates indicate that if clusters do exist, they account for less than 5 percent of teen suicides. Thus, even if it is valid, the idea of clusters has only limited use in helping us understand how and why teenagers choose to kill themselves.

Perhaps the cluster effect is important within a closed society, such as a boarding school or a summer camp. Perhaps it is also important in a particular high school, if students react to friends' and classmates' self-imposed deaths with depression and isolation, experiences that can intensify suicidal feelings. As we try to understand why and how people reach the decision to end their own lives, however, we must look beyond the simple "copycat" effect or the "cluster" syndrome to the deeper truths about suicide.

A Social Perspective

Why is the rate of teen suicide going up so quickly in America? In the next few chapters, we'll look at some of the psychological reasons behind suicide-but psychology doesn't explain everything. It doesn't tell us why some societies have a particularly high teen suicide rate while others have a far smaller problem. The differences in teen suicide rates suggest that different social structures, cultures, religions, child-rearing practices, and ways of thinking can have different impacts on a teenager's decision to commit suicide—or to avoid doing so.

Historically, different religions have had different attitudes about suicide. Judaism and Christianity both made suicide a sin. According to both religions, only God can give life, so only God should be able to take it away. The commandment "Thou shalt not kill" is seen to apply both to murder and to suicide. Following this thinking, many Christian-influenced countries actually made suicide against the law. As late as 1969, according to *Teenage Suicide* by Sandra Gardner with Gary Rosenberg, M.D., a teenager on the Isle of Man, off Great Britain, was actually "birched"—beaten— in punishment for a suicide attempt.

In Japan, on the other hand, there is no blanket religious injunction against suicide, which is seen as an honorable choice in some situations, one that is preferable to undergoing certain kinds of shame. This cultural difference, along with the enormous amount of stress and competition endured by Japanese teenagers, helps to make the Japanese teen suicide rate one of the highest in the world. According to Dr. Mamoru Iga, cited in *Teenage Suicide*, Japanese teenagers undergo a particularly high degree of stress from the competitive examinations that they must all take, exams that determine what kind of education and career future they may look forward to. A Japanese high school student who does not do well on exams may see death as preferable to living with poor results.

The authors of *Teenage Suicide* speculate that another factor contributing to high teen suicide in Japan is the strong emphasis on family respect. Japanese teenagers are not supposed to show anger, and they are particularly instructed to avoid showing anger against their parents. A young person in Japan who feels upset at his or her parents' pressure to succeed in examinations may come to believe that the only outlet for his or her feelings is suicide.

The cultural prescription against anger seems to be a reason for the high teenage suicide rate in Truk, a Micronesian island group where among males 15 to 24, there are 25 suicides per 10,000. Sociologists speculate that Truk teenage boys are suffering from the Westernization of their society, which has produced many swift and often unpleasant changes. The combination of the traditional injunction against anger and the new undermining of community support may have produced feelings of anger, frustration, and despair that young people take out on themselves, rather than expressing in some other way.

What about in America? Why would the teenage suicide rate be going up so quickly in this country? Although no one really knows the answer to this question, many experts—sociologists, psychologists, historians, and others—have suggested possible reasons.

First, as we've seen, is the increasing mobility of American society since World War II—that is, the greater tendency for families to move out of one community into another. Judie Smith, says that the experience of loss is extremely traumatic for teenagers—and making a move certainly represents a number of losses: of one's room, one's friends, one's boyfriend or girlfriend, one's school and teachers, one's neighborhood and community. As Smith says:

> The major factor, the common thread [among teens who attempt suicide] is the experience of loss. These kids have lost friendships, ties—it's a traumatic upheaval when a child is moved from one community to another . . . . once they get through this and there's another loss, like a breakup of a relationship with a boyfriend or girlfriend, it's an added crisis. These kids haven't had the life experience to get over it.

Other experts point to increased pressures on teenagers to get involved in sexual relationships that they may not be ready to handle. Both the emotional pressures of an intense romantic relationship and the possible consequences of such a relationship—such as a sexually transmitted disease or a pregnancy—can increase teenage stress. Dr. Sol Gordon, an expert on teen sexuality, believes that pregnancy or the fear of being pregnant is the single biggest factor in teenage girls' suicide attempts or acts. Gordon says that when girls feel abandoned by their boyfriends and their families, they may believe that have nowhere to turn—and so death seems like the only solution.

Although homosexuality is increasingly more accepted by our society, there is still a great deal of pressure on teenagers to be straight rather than gay. As Gordon says, "People have reported incidents of young men attempting or actually committing suicide because of fears of homosexuality. . . . It's a heavy trip for boys, since it's considered such a stigma." In such a climate, someone who believes that he or she is gay may be driven by fear or despair to consider suicide as an alternative—even though most gay people, like most heterosexual people, actually lead happy and satisfying lives.

Dr. Harold Treffert, director of the Winnebago Mental Health Institute of Oshkosh, Wisconsin, also cites cultural reasons for teenage suicide. He says, "A lot of teenage suicides are the result of the 'American Fairy Tale,'" which he defines as follows: "More possessions means happiness; a person who produces is more important; everyone must belong to or identify with a larger group; perfect mental health means no problems; a person is abnormal unless he or she is constantly happy." Such a climate is certainly supported by television, which bombards teenagers with images of happy, beautiful, and well—dressed young people, fairy-tale teenagers who seem to have all the possessions they want, all the friends they need, unlimited love from their families, and the ability to solve all their problems in 30, 60, or at most 120 minutes. Since real life rarely if ever measures up to this media portrait, it's easy for teenagers—and adults!—to lose perspective on their own lives, feeling like failures because they can't measure up to impossible standards.

Myths and Facts About Suicide

One of the problems in dealing with suicide among any age group is that there are so many myths about it. While there are many aspects of suicide that cause experts to disagree, experts *can* be sure of some basic facts. Do you know what they are? On another sheet of paper, take the following myth/fact quiz to see if you can tell the difference between what's true and false when it comes to suicide.

_____ 1.   People who talk about suicide never follow through.
_____ 2.   If you talk about suicide with someone who's depressed, you might be giving the person the idea yourself.
_____ 3.   When a person who's been depressed for a long time seems to cheer up, that is often a bad sign.
_____ 4.   Suicides are usually spontaneous, spur-of-the-moment decisions.
_____ 5.   April is the month with the highest suicide rate.
_____ 6.   People are more likely to kill themselves when the weather is gloomy and rainy than on a bright, sunny day.
_____ 7.   Most people who commit suicide are crazy.
_____ 8.   If a person is rescued from a suicide attempt, he or she usually doesn't try again.
_____ 9.   Regular people don't usually commit suicide—there is a certain type who does.
_____10.   If someone is really determined to commit suicide, there's not much that can be done to stop the person.

What did you think? Compare your answers with the ones below.

1. People who talk about suicide never follow through.—Myth. According to Margaret O. Hyde and Elizabeth Held Forsyth, M.D., authors of *Suicide: The Hidden Epidemic*, some studies say that 60 to 80 percent of all suicides gave some kind of indication of their intentions. A person might talk openly about wanting to commit suicide. Or a suicidal person might speculate about what happens after you die, or joke about suicide, or talk seriously or casually about another person who also committed suicide. He or she might wonder what life will be like after he or she is gone, or talk about the kind of funeral he or she wants. Generally, preoccupation with suicide, death, and life after death might be a clue that a person is thinking about committing suicide. If a person talks openly about suicide, he or she may be considering it. Everyone who talks about suicide should be listened to carefully, particularly someone who has been depressed or who has just suffered a loss or disappointment.

2. If you talk about suicide with someone who's depressed, you might be giving the person the idea yourself.—Myth. Experts agree that it's better to talk openly about suicide with someone who seems depressed or upset, rather than avoiding the subject. If the person is not interested in suicide, nothing you say will get him or her interested. If the person is considering suicide, talking about the subject may give him or her the chance to explore feelings and maybe get help. In fact, experts recommend that if a person seems extremely depressed or discouraged, a friend might say, "I'm worried to hear you talk that way, because it sounds like you might be thinking about killing yourself or something like that." If the person is considering suicide, this might be an opening to talk about the problem rather than follow through with the suicide.

3. When a person who's been depressed for a long time seems to cheer up, that is often a bad sign.—Fact. Ironically, a person who has seemed to reach a kind of peace or contentment after a long period of depression may actually be feeling relieved: He or she has finally decided to commit suicide, and that decision brings a certain kind of relief.

Sometimes, too, a person who has felt immobilized by depression feels a surge of energy when he or she finally starts to recover. The depression has led to a state of inertia: to the feeling that the person isn't capable of doing anything more than dragging through the next moment or isn't able to plan any further ahead than the next hour or so. When the depression recedes somewhat, the person may feel the energy to plan or to take action—and, sadly, may then wish to take action to end his or her life.

A person whose suicidal feelings are related to *schizophrenia*, a form of mental illness, may not be able to think clearly or rationally while the schizophrenia is most intense. When the irrational thoughts and feelings recede somewhat, the person may then be capable of rational planning—and may then choose to commit suicide.

The sad thing is that suicide—the ending of a life and of all the possibilities that go with it—might seem like a "rational" choice to someone. The depressed person might feel so helpless or hopeless about life that the only positive action that seems within reach is the action to end life itself.

4. Suicides are usually spontaneous, spur-of-the-moment decisions.—Myth. A person who commits suicide rarely has come to this decision without some kind of planning or forethought. Usually a person has fantasies of what the suicide will be like. Perhaps the fantasies take the form of careful planning of how the death will take place. Perhaps they take the form of imagining how everyone will feel afterward—sorry they didn't value the person more, or loving toward the absent person, or miserable and guilty about the suicide. They may be fantasies about how peaceful death will be or of how wonderful a life after death will seem. Whether the person's plans or fantasies concern the suicide itself, its aftermath, or the idea of death, the person who commits or attempts suicide usually does so with a long history of preparation.

By knowing these facts, people have greater chance of realizing when a friend or a relative is considering suicide and therefore a greater chance of intervening. That's why experts believe it's helpful to talk about suicide with someone who seems extremely depressed or unusually preoccupied with thoughts of death. Encouraging the person to talk about his or her plans or fantasies, rather than keeping them secret, can serve as a kind of safety valve, where the person has a chance to realize that death really *won't* solve the problems of life. It also gives others a chance to offer help and act to prevent the suicide.

5. April is the month with the highest suicide rate.— Fact. Ironically, the coming of spring and, in most places, better weather can actually make the potential suicide feel worse. The person may have hoped or believed that better weather would improve his or her spirits. When it doesn't, it may seem as if *nothing* will help. The person may also feel resentful or isolated because other people seem to be happy and excited about the springtime, while he or she still feels helpless and hopeless. Spring is a symbol of hope, so if the gap between the "hopeful" outside world and the "hopeless" inner state seems too great, a person may think suicide is the way to resolve the conflict.

Some people may have heard the myth that December is the month with the highest suicide rate, since people have high expectations of family togetherness that, if not met, are extremely disappointing. Actually, writing in *Suicide: The Hidden Epidemic*, Margaret O. Hyde and Elizabeth Held Forsyth, M.D. point out that *homicide* rates actually go up in December in some states, since family stresses may provoke people to violence against other family members. Hyde and Forsyth speculate that the sense of belonging, even to a difficult family, seems to mitigate against suicide, however, and that the sense of belonging generally extends into community "good feelings, even with strangers."

Of course, every person's decision is individual, and we are only talking about averages here. Any individual might decide to commit suicide during any month—or might be helped to decide *not* to commit suicide at any time.

6. Suicides are more likely to kill themselves when the weather is gloomy and rainy than on a bright, sunny day.—Myth. As we've just seen, suicide is connected to feeling isolated, so that a suicidal person might actually feel less isolated on a gloomy day when everyone else is also feeling low. To a person who feels depressed and isolated, a bright day may seem like one more proof that he or she can't enjoy the same things as everybody else.

This reasoning also helps explain why it isn't helpful to tell a depressed person, "You have no reason to feel depressed—look at all the good things in your life!" If a person is feeling depressed, he or she may not be able to enjoy those good things. Knowing that other people *can* enjoy them might make a depressed person feel even more isolated and helpless—the feelings that contributed to the desire for death in the first place.

Some studies have shown that people are generally more prone to suicide if they live in areas where the days are short and the nights are long, or places where the climate is especially rainy and cloudy (even if the person does not pick a bad-weather day for the actual suicide). These studies draw on theories claiming that depriving a person of sunlight increases the likelihood of depression. However, according to Hyde and Forsyth, "Various kinds of weather have been accused of increasing the number of suicides, but statistics vary so greatly that it is impossible to draw any useful conclusions."

7. Most people who commit suicide are crazy.— Myth. Of course, the definition of "crazy" is a tricky one. But if we define a "crazy" person as someone who is really out of touch with reality to the point where he or she has difficulty functioning, then we see that most suicides are not "crazy" most of the time. They may be able to lead apparently normal, even successful lives—up until the moment they decide to end their lives. There may be a terrible, painful gap between what they are feeling and the way their lives look to others, but they certainly are not "crazy" or unable to keep their lives together most of the time.

Some suicides are "crazy"; that is, they would be diagnosed with a severe mental illness that keeps them from functioning at the level reached by most people their age. A person with schizophrenia, for example, might hear voices or see visions that are not really there. He or she might suffer from the *delusion* that objects or animals are talking to him or her, giving instructions for suicide or for self-destructive behavior. Many experts now hold the theory that schizophrenia has its source in an imbalance in brain chemistry, although emotional factors may be involved also. As we saw, a schizophrenic may actually wait to attempt suicide until he or she is feeling better and more capable. Ironically, the person, may believe he or she is taking the only action possible to escape the often painful effects of the schizophrenia. The writer Virginia Woolf left a suicide note explaining that she was killing herself because she couldn't bear the thought that her hallucinations were beginning again.

If only "crazy" people commit suicide, the problem would be much easier to solve because we can usually tell that someone has a mental illness by many other ways than suicidal behavior. Identifying mentally ill people is much easier than knowing which "normal" people may turn to suicide. Sadly, many types of pain can be very easy to hide from others, and the pain of someone who thinks about taking his or her own life might or might not be visible to other people. Friends of the writer Anne Sexton, for example, claim that they had no idea that she was intending to commit suicide. In fact, the last person she saw before she took her life was her friend the writer Maxine Kumin, with whom she had just had lunch. Kumin later wrote several poems about how sad, angry, and betrayed she felt that her friend had given her no sign of her deep distress.

8. If a person is rescued from a suicide attempt, he or she usually doesn't try again.—False. Although many people who make one suicide attempt never try again, other people try several times, either during a single period or at various times throughout their lives. For those who try only once, the attempt may have resolved some conflict they felt or may have gotten them the help they needed. Those who try more than once may have many reasons for their repeated attempts.

In some cases, people never mean their repeated suicide attempts to succeed. Rather, they are a way of asking for help—a way that backfires when the suicide attempt becomes an actual suicide. The writer Sylvia Plath, for example, staged a suicide attempt by turning on the gas oven in her London apartment just before a servant was supposed to arrive. Plath even left a note for the servant, telling her which doctor to call and giving her the doctor's number. However, the gas leaked into the apartment of the downstairs neighbor, causing him to pass out—so that he could not let in the servant. By the time anyone reached Plath's apartment, she had died—although she had clearly planned to be rescued. Plath had attempted suicide as a young girl, and scholars today speculate that she may have seen this act as a symbolic way of taking control of her own life, as if life after the suicide attempt was somehow "new." Sadly, Plath never had a chance at her new life, even though she clearly wanted one.

Other repeat suicide attempts may reflect a person's genuine wish to die, a wish that for some reason was frustrated in an earlier attempt. Repeated attempts may also reflect recurring depression, so that a person turns to suicide whenever the overwhelming feelings of depression return.

Of course, many people can be helped by intervention, either before or after a suicide attempt, and these people never attempt suicide again. A person might also make repeated attempts before he or she has finally resolved the problems that led to them. Since some people do make repeated attempts, however, no one should automatically assume that a rescued suicide survivor will not try to commit suicide again.

9. Regular people don't usually commit suicide—there is a certain type who does.—Myth. Suicide cuts across all lines of class, race, and gender. Rich and poor, working class and middle class, black and white, Asian and Hispanic, Native American and European American, male and female, young and old—there is no one "type" of person whom we can identify as a "suicidal type." Sadly, this way of dealing with one's problems exists among all types of people in every society.

It's true that there may be some statistical differences among groups within a society. For example, women are more likely to attempt suicide than men, and men are more likely to be successful. However, the numbers of men and women who attempt and commit suicide are high enough that it is not possible to say that "a certain type" does or doesn't do this.

Likewise, there may be some societies where suicide rates are higher or lower, or where suicide rates change over time. A society's attitudes about death, individual rights, child rearing, the future, religion, and many other factors may influence whether many or few of its members make this sad choice. However, in American society in the 1990s, it isn't possible to say that any one group of people is the "type" to commit suicide.

10. If someone is really determined to commit suicide, there's not much that can be done to stop the person.—Myth. Fortunately, the good news about suicide is that it *can* be prevented. As we have seen, often a person who is considering suicide will talk about the decision, directly or indirectly, or will leave warning signs in some other way. While it is not always possible to read these signs or to act upon them, frequently it is possible. Many people have reported being helped by counseling, by suicide hot lines, by crisis centers, by friends and family members, or even by strangers.

Sometimes the only intervention that's needed is for someone to say "Please don't." Sometimes it takes years of counseling, even hospitalization. There is a whole range of options in between. In later chapters, we'll talk about ways that individuals can help people who are considering suicide, as well as the kinds of options and interventions that may be available in your community. For now, however, let us stress that while no one should feel guilty about not preventing a suicide that has already taken place, everyone can feel optimistic about the possibility of preventing a suicide in the future.

Thinking about Teenage Suicide

As we have seen, teenagers actually have a lower suicide rate than many other age groups. Yet studies show that many teenagers spend a great deal of time preoccupied with suicide, whether or not they actually attempt or complete the act itself. A 1991 study conducted by the Centers for Disease Control, covering 886 students at 10 randomly selected New York City high schools, found that 29.3 percent of the students surveyed had considered suicide during the past year. Some 18.4 percent had gone so far as to make plans for their suicides, and 8.2 percent had attempted suicide at least once.

These suicide attempts may represent more of a cry for help than an actual determination to end a life: Only 1.8 percent of the students questioned in this survey reported that their attempts had resulted in an "injury, poisoning, or overdose that had to be treated by a doctor or nurse." Yet the very fact that young people would choose to express their distress and frustration in such a violent and self-wounding way reveals a painful crisis among teens.

What problems drive teenagers to consider killing themselves? Researchers Diane de Anda and Melanie A. Smith examined data on 165 adolescents (ages 12 to 19), 65 young adults (ages 20 to 26), and 175 adults (ages 27 and older) who called two suicide help lines in Los Angeles County during a two-week period. The survey, published in the July 1993 issue of *Social Work*, found that teenagers have quite different reasons for calling suicide hot lines than do young adults or adults. Whereas depression was the major reason that young adults and adults considered suicide (29.2 percent and 32.6 percent, respectively), most teenagers who called the hot lines studied did not report depression as a problem (only 5.4 percent). Likewise, loneliness or lack of a relationship was frequently reported by young adults (26.2 percent) and adults (29.7 percent), whereas few teenagers reported either of these reasons as why they were thinking about suicide (only 6.0 percent).

On the other hand, problems in love relationships were frequently cited by suicidal teens (20.6 percent), as were family problems and conflicts (16.4 percent). Of course, figures may be somewhat skewed by the fact that the vast majority—70.3 percent—of the teenage callers were female. Females are generally far more likely to ask for help when they are experiencing problems, even though, as we have seen, males of all ages have a higher suicide rate.

Still, the fact that teenagers have their own reasons for committing suicide is significant.

It further points up the fact that when teenagers consider suicide, they are far less likely than adults to be expressing the idea that they wish to *end* their lives. They are more likely to be considering suicide as a means to *solve the problems* of their lives. Although it's sad that the ending of a life would ever seem to be a solution to life's problems, understanding this dynamic leaves room for hope: If a troubled teen comes to see another way to solve his or her problems, suicide can cease to be an option.

Thinking about suicide may be painful and disturbing—but it may also open the door to new understanding. For many years, suicide was considered an unthinkable act. People who committed suicide were seen as first immoral, then criminal, and finally insane. Now we understand that anyone *might* consider suicide as a "solution" to life's problems, even though not everyone *does*. The more we understand about suicide, the more freely we are able to talk about it, the better chance we have at penetrating its mystery.

2

Why Do People Do It?

Maria has been holding it together for a while. Then she has a fight with Luce, her best friend. It's just a stupid misunderstanding—they were supposed to meet downtown at a fast-food place, but Maria got mixed up and waited at home for Luce to come get her. Luce waited for two hours, and when she finally called, she yelled at Maria, "How could you be so stupid! I don't need this! You think you can just keep me waiting around like that?"

Luce and Maria have had fights before, and any other time, Maria would know this is just Luce blowing off steam. But somehow, this time, the fight really gets to Maria. She feels like she's lost her last friend—and it's all her fault. She feels so stupid and ugly that she can hardly stand it. "No one will ever really care about me again—I really blew it," she tells herself. Suddenly, all she can think about is getting out the razor blade and this time, really using it.

When Charles gets the D on his chemistry test, it seems to send him into a tailspin. On the surface, everything is okay. He's still getting good grades in the rest of his classes. He and his parents are still getting along; his friends and his girlfriend don't notice any problems.

Inside, though, he feels like a fraud. Sometimes he thinks, "If they knew what I was really like, they wouldn't care about me any more." Other times he thinks, "They do know what I'm like—and they're the ones putting on an act, pretending to care about me." Either way, he feels like he's living "on borrowed time"—that sooner or later, everyone will treat him like the disgusting failure that he is. Charles feels like someone has pulled one thread—and now his whole life has just unraveled. It's as if his whole life is already over and there's nothing he can do about it.

Evie feels as if she's just drifting along surrounded by a thick, gray cloud. The cloud seems to be inside her as well, turning all her feelings into blank, blah nothing. Sometimes she sits in her room alone, crying over a piece of music, something she read, or just nothing at all. Sometimes she just sits, not crying, not really upset, just feeling empty. Lately it seems as if she doesn't even have the energy to drag herself from home to school and back. Yet even though she's always tired, she's having trouble sleeping. She doesn't feel like eating anything, yet she often feels hungry.

Evie's mother seems to notice that something is wrong. A few times she's asked her daughter if everything is all right, but when Evie says, "Oh, sure, Mom," her mother seems to believe her and backs off. When her favorite English teacher invites Evie to have coffee with her after school one day and talk about poetry, Evie makes some excuse about having to go shopping with her mother. Really, she feels too tired to talk to anyone and she'd rather just go home. Sometimes, Evie thinks, all she really wants to do is just sleep and sleep and never wake up.

The Trigger Event

Teenage suicide and suicide attempts are frequently set off by a particular incident, known to psychologists as a *trigger event*. Sometimes this event may seem quite small and trivial to others, such as Maria's fight with her friend. Sometimes this event may seem more serious, such as Charles's D in chemistry. Sometimes the trigger event may be quite serious, such as the death of a relative or a divorcing parent's move to another city. However serious or trivial this event seems to others, though, the incident takes on tremendous importance to the person considering suicide. If we understand how people reach the decision to kill themselves, we might begin by understanding the nature of the trigger event.

Generally, a suicide is set off by some kind of loss or failure. The following are all examples of events that a person might experience in this way:

- A parent's death, abandonment, or divorce
- A breakup with a boyfriend or girlfriend
- The loss of a friend through a fight, a move to another city, or simply growing apart
- A move to another city, isolating the person from friends or family
- A failure in sports, schoolwork, or the arts, such as a lost game, a poor grade, or an unsuccessful recital or play
- An injury that puts an end to hopes for a career in sports, music, or dance
- The loss of a job or the failure to get a job that the person had hoped for
- The failure to win a contest of some kind
- A disappointment of anything that had been particularly hoped for

Why does the trigger event seem so devastating? Sometimes it represents the loss of something that a teenager had pinned all of his or her hopes on. For example, if a girl is insecure about herself, she might feel that she isn't worth anything if she can't get a boy to love her. When she gets a boyfriend, she pins all her hopes on him. He is not just someone to enjoy being with, he is the proof that she is a good, lovable person. If she feels this way, a boyfriend breaking up with her, or even having a fight with her, might make the girl feel hopeless about ever being loved by anyone. Instead of being able to bounce back, saying "I miss Jed, but I'll find someone else someday," the girl might think, "This just proves what I've always known—I'm worthless and awful and everybody can tell how creepy I am."

In the same way, if a boy feels lonely and unsure of himself, losing a girlfriend might confirm all of his worst fears. He may have put all his hopes into the relationship, thinking "This is it, I've finally found the girl of my dreams. She's the person who will keep me from being lonely." Then, if they break up or have a difficult period, the boy isn't likely to think "I wish Gina still wanted to go out with me—I guess I'm in for a lonely month or two." Instead, he says to himself, "I managed to fool one person into loving me, but now that's all over. I tricked her, but I can't trick anyone else—I'm just not much of a man."

A person like Charles, who feels a strong need to do well at everything and to have everyone like him, might be easily thrown by even a small failure, such as a bad grade. Another person might see a D as a bad break, or a small mistake, or even as a sign that he'll never be good at chemistry—but so what, because there are plenty of other things that he might be good at. Charles sees a D in chemistry as a sign that his worst fears are true, that he really *isn't* good at anything, that everything is going to crumble now that the first thing has gone wrong.

You might say that the trigger event feels bigger than it is because it seems to stand for so much more than itself. A lost love isn't just one person, it's everybody who will ever love the person, ever. A bad experience isn't just a tough time, it's proof that nothing in life will ever be right. A failure isn't just a single obstacle, it's confirmation that the person will fail and fail and fail, for the rest of his or her life.

People have often been surprised by the seemingly minor nature of some trigger events. A girl is upset over having to wear braces, a boy is mad because he's not allowed to watch a special program on television. A high school freshman is disappointed over not getting a Valentine, a junior high school student was turned down for a date. Parents, friends, and classmates who remember these events wonder, "Why was *that* so important?" As A. Alvarez, himself an attempted suicide, wrote in *The Savage God*, such events "are like a trivial border incident which triggers off a major war." The accumulated stresses and sorrows of everything that came before are ready to explode—all it takes is one more disappointment.

Of course, sometimes a trigger event really *is* devastating, by anybody's standards. The death of a parent, relative, or friend is a genuinely shattering experience. No one takes such an event lightly; most teenagers who experience the death of a loved one feel overwhelmed by grief and marked by long-lasting pain.

Likewise, when parents divorce, most teenagers feel that, in some sense, their world has fallen apart. Even if the parents hadn't been getting along well, it's still upsetting to face the breaking up of one's household. Most children hold on to the fantasy that someday their parents will work out their problems and become a happy, devoted couple; divorce puts a definite end to that fantasy, which virtually everybody finds painful. Furthermore, a divorce often disrupts teenagers' lives in profound and upsetting ways; it sometimes causes a family to move and often means that the child sees less of a beloved parent.

Yet many teenagers go through a death or divorce without considering suicide, even if they are overwhelmed by pain or anger. Likewise, a rape or an assault may be an especially painful trigger event—but most people who are hurt in this way do not respond by ending their own lives. What turns these tragedies into an occasion for suicidal feelings or behavior?

When Stress Piles Up

Sometimes the trigger event is just the latest in a series of stressful events. The accumulation of stress makes it difficult for some people to "bounce back" from difficulties or from tragedies. If too many stressful events take place in too short a time, our defenses are weakened and our resources depleted. Under such circumstances, an event that might otherwise seem trivial becomes a major disaster; a genuine tragedy may seem virtually unbearable.

Maria's fight with her friend becomes a trigger event because of the accumulated stress that Maria feels. If Maria were having a great year, she could bounce back from a fight with Luce without thinking much about it. If she were relaxed and happy, she would remember that Luce often blows up over little things and then forgets all about it afterward. She might decide that she doesn't like this quality in Luce, but she wouldn't let it get to her. Even if she decided to see less of Luce, or to stop being Luce's friend, she wouldn't feel that she was the one who was unlovable. In other words, she would be able to keep things in perspective.

But because Maria is already feeling stretched to the limit, she loses her perspective and overreacts. Instead of seeing Luce's outburst as Luce's problem, she takes it as a sign that she, Maria, will never have any friends. In order to understand why Maria isn't thinking clearly, we need to understand a little more about stress.

What Is Stress?

Stress is any event in our lives that forces us to adjust or adapt. Sometimes stress can be caused by a happy event, such as falling in love or winning a scholarship. Sometimes it can be caused by a difficulty, such as the loss of a friend or a move to another city. Stress can even be caused by having nothing exciting going on in one's life—which produces the unpleasant need to adjust to boredom!

Whatever the source, stress puts a strain on our resources. Of course, adjusting and adapting to various events is part of life. But when there are too many adjustments or difficult adaptations to make in too short a time, sometimes the system overloads.

In 1967, the scientists T. H. Holmes and R. H. Rahe developed a list of several dozen events that could cause stress in a person's life—that is, events that require a person to make a big or a small change. The chart was originally developed for adults. Here's a list of stressful events adapted to apply to teenagers:

Stressful Events

- Death of a parent or close family member
- Breakup with a boyfriend or girlfriend
- Going to jail
- Personal injury or illness
- Starting a new relationship
- Trouble at school
- Getting back together with a boyfriend or girlfriend
- Falling in love
- Starting a new relationship
- Losing a job
- Changing schools
- Graduating (or moving from middle school to junior high, or from junior high to high school)
- Getting pregnant
- Trouble with sex or relationships
- A new person joining the household—for example, the birth of a new brother or sister, or a new person coming to live with the family
- Starting a new year at school

- New requirements at school or in one course
- Change in financial state—a lot worse off or a lot better off than usual
- Death of a close friend
- Loss of a close friend
- Starting a new school activity
- A change in the number of arguments with family or boyfriend/girlfriend—either a lot fewer or a lot more than usual
- Changes in allowance or other financial changes
- Change in responsibilities at home—more or less housework, baby-sitting, and so on
- Someone leaving home—through divorce, going away to college, living elsewhere for another reason
- Outstanding personal achievement—in school, sports, or the arts
- Someone at home starts a new job or loses a job
- A change in living conditions—a move, remodeling the house, or a change in the neighborhood
- Changing your personal habits—dressing differently, hanging out with different people
- Change in church activities, social activities, or other recreation
- Change in sleeping habits—sleeping a lot more or a lot less, or sleeping on a diffferent schedule
- Change in the number of family get-togethers
- Change in eating habits—eating a lot more, a lot less, on a different diet, or on a different schedule
- Vacation
- Holidays
- Minor violations of the law, such as a traffic ticket

As you can see, some of these events are sad ones, representing death, loss, or unpleasant changes. Other events, however, are happy ones—falling in love, getting back together with someone, taking a vacation, suddenly having *more* money to spend. Whether stressful events are happy or sad, however, they all have one thing in common: They require a person to adapt to change. In addition, for reasons that we will explore in Chapter 3, many people find happy events even more stressful than sad ones. Some people are so used to expecting bad things to happen, they almost feel safe when things are going as badly as they expect. Then, if things get better, they feel worried and anxious—when are the bad things that they expect going to start happening again?

For people who see the world this way, disappointments that follow good times are especially devastating. That's partly because the good times were so stressful—so full of worry about when the bad times were going to come back—that when something bad happens, the person has very few resources left to cope with it. Also, bad times and disappointments—which, after all, happen to everybody—come to seem like a punishment for ever having fun. They seem like a reminder that the person should never expect anything in his or her life to be good, as if such an expectation will always bring a terrible punishment. A person who sees the world this way might then decide that life is not worth living. After all, if bad times are the rule and good times only bring punishments and disappointments, what is there in life to look forward to?

What are the accumulated stresses in Maria's life?

- Although her parents split up when she was 10, they never actually got divorced until last year, when she was 14.
- Also last year, Maria's mother got a new boyfriend who started living with the family—meaning a new person had joined the household.
- Ever since the new boyfriend moved in, Maria's father has been staying away—loss of a parent (through divorce, not death).
- This is Maria's first year in high school—a change of schools.

- Maria's mother recently got laid off from her job so her family doesn't have much money these days—a change in financial status.
- Maria hasn't been doing well at school, and she already feels her teachers don't like her—trouble at school.

Each of these situations has required Maria to adapt, to change, or to defend herself against difficulties. Each of these situations has taken a little bit more of her energy. All it takes is one more source of stress—the fight with Luce—to make Maria feel that she just can't handle so many problems.

In addition, the month before her fight with Luce, Maria had to adjust to some stress from a situation that was both happy and sad. Although she had been out with various guys, she had never really had a steady boyfriend that she liked. Actually, she thought that guys were trouble, that you couldn't trust them and you shouldn't give them a chance to hurt you. Then she met Tony, and everything seemed to change. Tony always called her at the beginning of the week to make dates for the weekend. At school, he would come to find her between classes, and he always made sure to eat lunch with her. He seemed really to like Maria, and although at first she didn't think much of him, the more she got to know him, the better she liked him. He kept telling her, "You've got to trust me, Maria, you've got to trust me," and she actually started thinking "Well, maybe I should trust him. Maybe he's not like other guys." Finally, Maria felt like she was really falling in love with Tony. For a couple of weeks, she was really happy. She felt she had finally found someone who loved her and cared about her, someone who treated her well and enjoyed being with her.

Then Tony stopped calling, and he started ignoring her in school. Maria was devastated. What had happened? She even called him once, but he just said, "Oh, nothing's wrong, but I've got to go now, Maria. I'll call you later," and then he never did. The next week, she saw him around school with another girl.

Even when Maria was happy with Tony, she was undergoing a lot of stress. She was having to change her ideas about how the world worked and what kind of person she was. From thinking that all guys were trouble and you couldn't trust any of them, she was starting to change her ideas to think that *this* guy was a good person and that maybe she could trust him. From thinking that no one would ever love her or be good to her, she was having to adjust to the idea that maybe somebody *could* love her and care about her.

Then, after she had started to make these stressful adjustments, she had another difficult change to go through—accepting the idea that now Tony didn't love her. Because it had been so hard for her to think that maybe a guy could really care about her, it was even more painful to accept that after all, no, he didn't. In fact, it felt as if Tony had left her *because* she had started to care about him and trust him. In Maria's way of thinking, this was the final proof. Once Tony had gotten to know her, he hadn't liked her—so obviously, no guy would ever like her. And, if she thought someone did care about her, she would get hurt even worse than if she firmly believed she was no good.

From the outside, we can see that Maria's way of thinking is not necessarily logical. Just because Tony didn't want to stay with her, that doesn't mean that no guy will ever like her again. Although Maria feels that Tony decided not to like her because she was so awful, we might think instead that *Tony* was the one who acted badly, encouraging Maria to trust him and then not being able to follow through. Either way, though, for Maria, the stress of being in love and being in a relationship, followed by the stress of being left and getting hurt, was a lot to handle. So when Luce has one of her little blowups, to Maria, it feels like a big blowup, because her sense of perspective has been so weakened by all the stress.

Of course, we all react to stress differently. Some people seem to have built-in stress management systems. They seem to be unusually well able to laugh off problems or to take things as they come. Other people are just built differently. They seem to have more sensitive systems, reacting more intensely to both the good times and the bad, hitting "higher highs" and "lower lows." Still other people vary greatly in their ability to handle stress. They may be cool about problems up to a certain point—and then suddenly they can't take it any more.

The amount of stress in itself doesn't predict how likely someone is to think about suicide. But accumulated stress may be a contributing factor. A series of adjustments and adaptations may put too much of a strain on a person's resources. Under those circumstances, either a minor snag or a major tragedy may feel like too much to bear. Some people handle this stress "overload" by getting sick. Other people simply get depressed. Still others find themselves angry over little things, or anxious, or just tired all the time. And some people react to an overload of stress by thinking about "ending it all"—through suicide or through some other violent act.

Depression

A trigger event may also set off a deeper sense of depression, a feeling that in turn may lead to suicidal feelings. However, not all suicidal people are depressed, and most depressed people never even consider suicide. In some people, however, depression may take the form of suicidal feelings and behavior. Evie is one of those people—her sense of misery leads her to feel like "sleeping and never waking up."

Depression can be hard to understand. We may confuse it with feeling sad, grieving, or having a hard time. Although people who are depressed may also have those other experiences, it's possible to be sad without being depressed— and it's possible to be depressed for no apparent reason, or for a reason that doesn't seem important enough to account for the depth and power of the depressed feelings.

Most psychologists think of depression as a feeling of helplessness and hopelessness, the feeling that nothing is right, with the world or with the person who is depressed, along with the sense that nothing will ever be right again. Many people feel depressed for short periods of time, particularly when they are teenagers—feeling blue or out of it or gloomy just seems to go with the territory. But when low spirits last longer than two weeks, or when they come back on a regular basis—say, a couple of days a week, every week—then depression becomes more serious.

We can identify three different types of depression. Sometimes depression is just a temporary case of the blues that occasionally bother everyone. Some depressions are set off by life events, such as a breakup with a boyfriend or girlfriend, the loss of a close friend, a parent's divorce or remarriage, or a move to another city. And some depressions—known as *major depression* or *clinical depression*—seem to hang on for a long time for no apparent reason.

No one has yet been able to fully explain this latter type of depression. Some doctors and psychiatrists believe that has psychological roots; others believe that it is caused by an imbalance in brain chemistry and/or hormones. In some cases, major depression may have both psychological and biological causes.

Depression often runs in families, for both biological and psychological reasons. To the extent that depression is caused by chemical imbalances, these may be passed on from parents to children, like many other aspects of body chemistry. To the extent that depression is psychological, a learned response to the world, children may learn it from their parents. If a girl sees her mother continually lying down with a "sick headache," she may decide that withdrawing from the world is the only reasonable way to cope with difficulties. If every time a father goes out with the family, he sits quietly by himself and doesn't say anything, his son may decide that that is just how men act.

In Evie's case, it was her father who was depressed. Evie's father was a salesman who got paid on commission. (That is, he got paid a percentage of the amount he sold.) He frequently worried about selling enough orders to take care of his family. Evie's father died when she was 10, but Evie has many memories of her father sitting alone in his bedroom, with none of the children allowed to go and talk to him because "Daddy is thinking hard right now." Evie picked up that when grown-ups had problems or concerns, they handled them by shutting themselves in their room, isolating themselves even from the people they are closest to.

Since depression is characterized by feeling helpless and hopeless, we can see how it might be set off by a triggering event of loss or failure. Maria's fight with Luce, for example, set off a larger feeling of depression—Maria's feeling that she's stupid and bad, that no one will ever care about her. Sometimes, as in Maria's case, depression is a reaction to stress, to the accumulated strains and difficulties that a person faces over time.

Sometimes, too, depression can refer back to an earlier event. In Maria's case, when Tony broke up with her, she was able to put up a good defense and act like it didn't matter to her. She shoved all her feelings out of the way, so that she really believed she didn't care. Then, when the fight with Luce happened, all of Maria's pain came rushing to the surface. It was as if the fight set free not just the feelings about Luce and her friendship, but also the feelings about Tony. And in a way, the feelings about Tony were also mixed up with Maria's feelings about her father's going away after the divorce, as well as all of the worry, fear, and sadness that came with the other big changes in her household. The triggering event had such force because it opened up many powerful feelings about many other important events.

In Evie's case, there doesn't seem to be any triggering event. She's been depressed for a long time; now it's getting worse. Perhaps this indicates that Evie's depression has biological roots, in her body chemistry or hormones; if so, her diet and exercise patterns may be making her depression worse. Or, possibly, her depression is just a by-product of the hormonal and body chemistry changes of adolescence.

On the other hand, perhaps Evie has deep psychological reasons for getting depressed and doesn't really need a "trigger event" to set her off. Her depression may be a reaction to her loneliness and isolation, as well as the way she learned to handle difficulty, a way she learned from watching her father.

Whether a person's depression has been set off by a triggering event or not, it can be recognized by the following signs:

- Less interest or no interest in things that the person used to enjoy, such as going to the movies, spending time with friends, or participating in sports
- Dramatic weight loss or gain
- Increased appetite or loss in appetite
- Sleeping far less or far more than usual; trouble sleeping or waking up
- A long-term loss of energy or sense of fatigue
- Feelings of worthlessness (in extreme cases, these are accompanied by delusions or hallucinations, such as feeling that one hears voices saying "You're no good.")
- Loss of interest in a physical relationship—or sudden interest only in the physical side of a relationship
- Frequent crying or being moved to tears very easily
- Headaches
- Lack of interest in one's physical appearance, or being overly preoccupied with physical appearance in a negative way
- Feeling as if the unpleasant emotions have always been there or as if they will never go away; not being able to imagine feeling any other way

Not everyone who is depressed feels all of these things, and many people who are not depressed feel some of them some of the time. But if you or someone you know feels *many* of these things *most of the time*, or *on a regular basis*, depression is probably the reason. As we've seen, Evie has many of the signs of depression: a "blah" feeling in which nothing gives her any pleasure, frequent crying, lack of energy, trouble sleeping, problems with appetite.

Masked Depression

Sometimes people who are depressed show it in other ways. This is known as *masked depression* and is most common in children and younger teenagers. Because depression is "masked" in these younger people, psychologists used to think that only adults and older teenagers got depressed. Now we know that anyone, of any age, can get depressed—and some psychologists even believe that, tragically, children as young as age three have tried to commit suicide.

Masked depression usually comes out as restlessness, tantrums, and fighting. In older teenagers, depression may also be masked with a lot of sexual acting out (sleeping around, putting oneself in risky sexual situations) or with risk-taking and reckless behavior (driving under the influence of drugs or alcohol, reckless driving in general, dares and stunts, and so on).

A person might show only the signs of masked depression. He or she also might show signs of both types of depression, combining recklessness, risk-taking, and fighting with problems in sleep and appetite or difficulty concentrating, for example.

Depression's Vicious Cycle

A depressed person may want to learn something more about the causes and treatments of depression, perhaps getting professional help to overcome this unpleasant condition. Unfortunately, part of the problem with depression is its vicious cycle. When you feel depressed, you feel hopeless, so you don't believe that anything will help you. The more hopeless you feel, the less likely you are to take action to get yourself the help you need—and the more depressed you will become.

Likewise, depressed people often feel isolated and lonely, even if they have many friends or a steady boyfriend or girlfriend. Evie shares that characteristic of depression. In her isolation, she feels that nothing anyone does can reach her. Even when her favorite teacher invites her to an event she would once have enjoyed—a discussion of books over coffee—Evie doesn't have the energy or the interest to go. Of course, the more she avoids people and things that once gave her pleasure, the more depressed she is likely to feel.

Depression and Suicide

As we've said, not everyone who is depressed feels suicidal, and many people who kill themselves are not depressed. Often, though, depression and suicide go together.

In Evie's case, they certainly do; she translates her feelings of sadness and loneliness into daydreams about how peaceful and happy her death will be and how many friends and loved ones it will draw to her. If thoughts of suicide or fantasies of death are part of someone's depression, that person is to some extent at risk for suicide.

According to George Howe Colt in *The Enigma of Suicide*, 70 percent of all suicides are associated with depression—although, of course, that means 30 percent are not. Colt also cites statistics showing that for every teenager who actually commits suicide, 1,000 more are depressed.

"I think that depression, in a funny way, is an inevitable part of adolescence," says psychiatrist Paul Walters, director of health services at Stanford University. "In fact, if you *don't* get depressed, I think there's something wrong."

When a teenager who has never been depressed before experiences depression for the first time, however, he or she may not know what is happening. These overwhelming feelings of sadness or lethargy may be frightening simply because they are new. And, while brief but intense episodes of depression are a normal part of growing up, to the person who's going through them, they don't seem "normal" and they don't seem "brief." If you don't know that your depression isn't going to last forever, you might indeed become desperate for a way to stop the pain.

Often, too, a person who is depressed believes that a certain single event will make everything better—a new boyfriend or girlfriend, summer vacation, an improved grade, a school or sports honor. When the hoped-for event actually happens and the depression continues anyway, the person may be overcome with the feeling that nothing in life works.

Teenage Changes

In the vast majority of cases, a person who is planning to commit suicide will leave clues. Likewise, a person who is at risk of suicide because of intense depression will show signs of his or her condition.

In the teenage years, however, these conditions—depression and vulnerability to suicide—are far more difficult to identify. That's because depression is such a big part of the teenage years. Changing bodies, raging hormones, new choices, greater responsibilities, increased family pressures, and the strains of breaking away from one's family can all combine to create conditions ripe for depression. As you can imagine, these rapid and dramatic occasions for adjusting and adapting are also quite stressful. Even a teenager who is not depressed may feel overwhelmed by all the new adjustments and adaptations he or she has to make. If parents are divorcing, remarrying, or making other changes in the household, the stress may accumulate.

Conflict with and about parents is another hallmark of the teenage years. Generally, as children we want our parents to take care of us. We want to look up to them and believe that they are powerful and strong, so that they will be better equipped to protect us. We want to think they are always right—or usually right!—so that we can learn from them. Even children from distressed families, even children from families that beat or abuse them, have this powerful need to have good and caring parents and to believe the best about their families.

Adolescence, though, is a time to begin separating from your parents. It's a time to start finding out what *you* think, who *you* are, what *you* can do. And how can you do that if your parents really are the wise and powerful people you used to think (or hope) they were?

To some extent, adolescents come into more conflict with parents simply because they are older and can see more clearly their parents' flaws and shortcomings—even if they don't want to. To some extent, however, teenagers need and want to see their parents' weaknesses, so that they will have the space to discover their own strengths. Whether you are currently getting along with your family or not, whether you had a happy childhood or a sad one, your teenage years will almost certainly include times of realizing the places where you and your parents differ and disagree. How else will you make yourself ready to go out and face the world as an adult?

Yet as much as most teenagers want that freedom and independence, they also want to know that someone is there and able to take care of them. That's what makes adolescence such a difficult time. Most teenagers want it both ways—they want to be independent and free, *and* they want to be protected and helped. The changes back and forth between those two feelings, or experiencing them both at the same time, is part of what makes the teenage years so confusing. This conflict can be painful, frustrating, confusing, or amusing, but whatever form it takes, it is a normal part of growing up.

In our society, these conflicts may be especially intense because teenagers get so many mixed messages. They aren't given adult earning power or sexual freedom; most teenagers in our society are not self-supporting, and most are not allowed to marry or even to have open sexual relationships. Yet they are expected to take a kind of adult responsibility for their futures in their schoolwork and their preparations for a job or college, and they are exposed to numerous sexual messages on television, at the movies, and in popular music.

Thus, a teenager who is trying to develop his or her own sense of purpose, to find his or her identity, may feel caught between the restrictions of childhood and the demands of adulthood. In this situation, it's hard to remember the truth: Sooner or later, you will be old enough to leave home, if you want to, and then you will have a chance to work these issues out. A person who can't see past the conflicts of adolescence might be tempted to end it all. But suicide—the ending of possibilities before they begin—might not seem so attractive if there is another, happier ending in sight.

The teen years can also intensify one of the worst aspects of depression—the sense that things are more terrible than they have ever been, and that they will never get better. Even adults who have lived through many periods of depression report difficulty in keeping their perspective while depressed. Despite experience to the contrary, while they are depressed they feel as if depression is all they have ever known and all they will ever know. If people can feel this way in the face of their own experience, imagine how much more vulnerable are teenagers, who do not have the life experience to assure them that depressions will in fact end someday. An adult may well be depressed at losing a loved one or failing at work, but he or she may have a wide enough range of experiences to help keep a sense of perspective about how serious the loss or the failure really is. Teenagers who break up with their boyfriend or girlfriend may be losing the first person with whom they were ever in love. How can they believe that the pain is only temporary—it *feels* as if it will last forever!

Likewise, an adult who experiences a failure may be depressed about it, but at least he or she might have the life experience to know that the failure is only one small piece of a much bigger puzzle. Teenagers who fail may have no way of knowing that they can also succeed—no way of putting their failure into perspective. As novelist George Eliot put it over 100 years ago, in youth, "Each crisis seems final, simply because it is new." In that view, suicide becomes a kind of "instant cure" to an "incurable" crisis—but, as one expert put it, that's like trying to treat a cold with a nuclear bomb.

Keeping one's perspective through stress and depression is a big challenge for people of any age. Learning what works for you, what helps you beat the blues, what helps you make it through a tough time, is part of what growing up is all about. It may be helpful to remember that going through difficult periods of depression or stress may actually be helping you to develop your resources for coping with life's ups and downs. Experiencing pain, disappointment, and loss is part of what makes us human; facing challenges and new situations is part of what makes life exciting and rewarding. Learning how we can best face life's demands can be an enriching part of the teenage years.

Coping with Stress and Depression

Everyone has his or her own methods of coping with stress and depression. Some methods are more successful than others. Which of the following methods do you recognize? Which work for you? Which don't? Are there any coping methods that you haven't yet tried, but that you think might be useful for you?

Effective Ways to Cope

- **Exercise**   Vigorous aerobic exercise—running, walking, swimming, dancing, exercise classes, basketball, handball, and racquetball—all provide a great release for stress and a good antidote to depression. Bicycling, while not considered an aerobic exercise, can be soothing and relaxing as well.
- **A healthy diet**   Sugar, caffeine, and fat deplete a person's resources. Although many people drink caffeinated beverages—coffee, tea, colas, hot chocolate—to wake themselves up or give themselves energy, sooner or later the high is always followed by a crash. Cutting down on these things and taking a recommended amount of vitamin B are good ideas.
- **A warm bath**   Making a private time when you can be alone in a pleasant place is a great way to relax or to soothe yourself. Try to find a time or make an arrangement with your family when you won't be interrupted.
- **Read**   Escaping into a good book can help you regain perspective or at least find release from your immediate troubles.
- **Spend time with people you care about**   Often during stressful periods, we might feel that we don't have time to just "be" with the people we enjoy; depressed people often tend to isolate themselves. Fight the isolation and reach out—it may make all the difference.
- **Write about what's bothering you**   Sometimes getting your thoughts out of your head and onto paper can help give you perspective or at least relief. Nothing is more worrisome or depressing than feeling the same thoughts chase each other around and around inside your head. Putting them down on paper can help you see them clearly instead of feeling vaguely upset or worried by them.
- **Give yourself a treat**   If you're feeling sad or worried about your life, remind yourself that there are good things within your grasp. Buy yourself a present, do something

nice for yourself, give yourself a little time off. You may find that you're better able to cope with even the busiest schedule or the most depressing situation after getting away from it for a while.

Ineffective Coping Methods

- **Drugs or alcohol**   Did you know that alcohol is actually a depressant? You might feel better while you're drunk or high, but afterward, you're almost sure to feel worse, especially if you're depressed. Drugs and alcohol might numb your painful feelings, but they don't make the feelings go away. (For more about where to get help with drug and alcohol problems, see Chapter 6.)
- **Binge or starve yourself**   Many people turn to food to help them cope with stress or depression. An occasional food treat or missed meal is no big deal, but if you are eating huge quantities of food or losing a great deal of weight, you are not coping with your problems—you are acting them out through your body. (For more about where to get help with food problems and eating disorders, see Chapter 6.)
- **Isolate yourself**   Sometimes the best way to cope with a hard day is to take some time by yourself to rest and recharge your batteries. But if you find that you are always alone, your isolation may actually be making things worse. Looking for ways to connect to people that you feel good about is likely to be more helpful than staying shut off from the world.

Of course, when we are feeling stressed out or depressed, that's often not the time we are able to reach out for help or do something nice for ourselves. That's the vicious cycle we talked about earlier: We feel stressed or depressed, we isolate or criticize ourselves, and then we feel more stressed out and even more depressed. In Chapter 4, we'll talk about ways to break this vicious cycle; in Chapter 6, we offer some specific resources—places to get help. For now, let's just repeat that stress and depression are a part of everyone's life. The challenge is for each of us to learn how we respond to these human conditions and to find the best methods for coping with them.

False Ideas and Wishful Thinking

So far we've looked at how stress, depression, and a trigger event of loss or failure might combine to get someone thinking about suicide. But we've also seen that everyone experiences stress, depression, and loss, so that by themselves, these may not be enough to explain why someone would choose to kill himself or herself.

Another component of suicidal thoughts and actions may be false beliefs or fantasies that teenagers may have about what death and suicide will mean. Although these beliefs are not logical or true, they may seem compelling at times, especially to a person who is feeling depressed or hopeless. These ideas may be based on *wishful thinking*—the practice of thinking that reality is the way you *wish* it would be, rather than the way it really is. Here are some common ideas that people who consider suicide may hold:

"They'll really be sorry now!"
Thinking of suicide as a form of revenge is very common among people who kill themselves. The person considering suicide imagines all the people who will feel guilty, regretful, or ashamed. For example, a boy who is mad at his parents for getting divorced may imagine that his suicide will make them sorry they didn't stay together and appreciate him while they had the chance. A girl who is angry at her boyfriend for leaving her may believe that he will feel guilty if she commits suicide. A student who is

failing a class may think that the teacher will feel punished for giving out that F.

Of course, the survivors may well feel all the guilt, shame, and regret that the suicide hopes they feel. What makes this belief false, however, is that the person who kills himself or herself won't be around to benefit from these feelings. A person might imagine the satisfaction of seeing friends, family, or teachers feeling miserable or upset—but if that person commits suicide, he or she *won't* see those people or feel any satisfaction at their pain. The suicide won't see or feel anything—he or she will be dead.

This view of suicide is actually based on a child's perception of death, not on an adult's grasp of reality. Think of the angry five-year-old who shouts at Mother, "I hate you, and I wish you were dead!" or "I'll kill you if you don't let me!" Does the child mean it? Yes—for that moment. Then the child wants Mother to come back to life and make peanut butter sandwiches for lunch. The idea that death is final and permanent is one that children below the age of 10 cannot really imagine. Saying "I wish you would die" doesn't mean "I never want to see you again," it means "*Right now*, I never want to see you again; in 10 minutes, I want you to come back and take care of me!"

In exactly the same way, imagining how sorry people will be after a suicide is leaving out the reality and the finality of death. Maybe the survivors *will* be just as miserable as the suicidal person hopes. But the person who has committed suicide won't be around to enjoy their regret.

"They'll have to do what I want!"
Using suicide to manipulate someone after death is a kind of variation of the revenge fantasy. People who leave suicide notes with explicit instructions about their wishes have probably experienced this particular fantasy. Although while they are alive they are frustrated that people don't seem to be following their wishes, they imagine that if they

kill themselves, they then will gain the power to make people do what they want.

As with the fantasy of revenge, this thought has elements of both truth and wishful thinking. A girlfriend, boyfriend, or family may well be so shattered by a suicide's death that they will do whatever they can to fulfill that person's last wishes. Yet even if they do, the person won't be around to enjoy this power or satisfaction. And of course, there's no guarantee that, even after death, the survivors will do what the suicide wanted. Imagine the case of a boy who leaves his ex-girlfriend a suicide note asking her to stop "cheating on him" with other guys. If the girl was not willing to see only this boy when he was alive and part of her life, imagine how much less willing she will be to stop seeing other guys now that her boyfriend is not even there. And because the boy is dead, there is now really nothing that he can do, either to win the girl back or to go on and make a happy life without her.

"They'll all come to my funeral—everyone will love me then."

In Mark Twain's *The Adventures of Tom Sawyer,* there is a scene in which Tom Sawyer's relatives and friends believe he is dead, although he has only run away. Tom sneaks back to attend the funeral they hold for him—and gets to hear everyone in town talking about what a good boy he was and how much they loved him. While he was around, everyone knew that Tom was a troublemaker, and they were often angry with him; now that he's gone, he's become the town saint.

Teenagers may well believe that in order for them to get the love and attention they need, they, like Tom, have to be at their own funerals. This fantasy may be supported by their experience with other teen suicides.

If these other teens are commemorated after their deaths with memorial services or special issues of the school paper, a classmate might well conclude that he or she should also die, just to get the attention.

Again, this idea of death is based on a false belief. The suicide won't be able to enjoy the praise and love that Tom Sawyer got to hear: Tom Sawyer was actually alive at his own funeral—but a person who commits suicide will be dead. We all want and need love and attention, but we can't enjoy it after we're dead.

"I'll be with him or her again."

One of the most powerful images of suicide is the fantasy of rejoining someone else who has died, especially someone else who has committed suicide. Accepting the loss of a loved one is very difficult. For a teenager, especially, losing a parent, a brother, or a sister can be devastating, and losing a friend, a boyfriend, or a girlfriend can bring overwhelming pain. As we just saw, it's very difficult for children to understand the finality of death. Teenagers, however, are old enough to grasp the reality that when people are dead, they are gone from this world forever. However true this may be, it's often quite painful to accept—so a person may develop the fantasy of somehow getting to see the loved one again, somewhere else.

If the person who died was also a suicide, then the image of somehow "following" him or her may be quite compelling. We'll explore those feelings more in Chapter 3, when we look at the experience of those who have survived suicides among family and friends. For now, let's just point out that wishful thinking is operating here too. No one knows for sure what happens after we die. Committing suicide is hardly a guarantee of being reunited with a person who has died. The idea of rejoining a person after death may be some kind of comfort to help us through a painful loss—but it's no assurance that suicide will let us rejoin that person.

Sometimes, too, the person who has died was someone we loved but not someone who treated us the way we wanted to be treated. Evie loved her father, but she was often frustrated at how he shut himself away from her. Most of the time she knew him, he was depressed—quiet, sad, preoccupied with his own problems and worries. Like every son or daughter, Evie really wanted her father to pay attention to her sometimes, to think she was wonderful and special, to feel happy and pleased just to be with her. Most times, though, this was not the relationship she had with him.

Now when Evie thinks about "going to sleep and never waking up," she also thinks about dying and getting to see her father again. But when Evie imagines rejoining her father, she doesn't picture the quiet, preoccupied man who ignored her. Instead, she pictures the loving father she always wanted. She imagines that, finally, her father will be happy to see her, that they will have the loving relationship she has always wanted with him. It's too painful for Evie to accept that she will never have this kind of relationship with her father, that she might never have had such a relationship with him even if he were still alive. Instead, she imagines a future where such a relationship might still happen—and then she believes that she must die to reach that future.

No matter how painful it is for Evie to accept reality, her fantasies won't bring her happiness either. She may wish that by killing herself, she could have a better relationship with her dead father, but if she follows through with her fantasy and kills herself, all she can be sure of is that she will be dead.

"I just want to end the pain."

At first glance, this type of thinking may seem less illogical. After all, sometimes people are in terrible pain, and such pain may well seem unbearable. We all have times when things hurt us deeply and nothing can ease or soothe our suffering. Certainly it's natural to want our pain to end and to imagine a time when we will be content and peaceful again.

Yet once again, wishful thinking is being used to make suicide seem like an end to pain. What we picture in our fantasies is not suicide—death, the absence of all feeling. Instead, we picture feeling *something*—peace, calm, contentment. Suicide won't create those feelings for us. Suicide will only make all of our feelings stop, forever, with the finality of death.

"Finally, I'll be taking charge of my own life."

One of the saddest reasons for committing suicide is the wish to take control of your life. People who feel that they are at the mercy of other people or circumstances may get to the point where it seems that the only power they have left is the power over their own lives. Sadly, they don't see any way to use this power to make their lives better. They can only imagine using their power to end their lives.

As with some of the other illogical ideas we've discussed, this idea has some truth in it, but in the end, it's based on a fantasy. The truth is that we are each responsible for our own lives. Whatever happens to us in the world around us, we always have some choice we can make, even if we aren't really happy with any of the choices. The idea of committing suicide to take control, however, is still based on the fantasy that we will feel *something* after control has been taken. We imagine feeling powerful, secure, determined, or sure of ourselves. In fact, people who decide to commit suicide may even feel some or all of these feelings. They may feel that, finally, they are taking a stand, making a choice, exercising power in their world.

The sad thing is, of course, that they experience these feelings *while* they are alive. The decision to commit suicide may indeed affect their feelings of power and control—but only while they are still alive to feel that way. After the suicide is complete, the feelings disappear because the person is dead. Their fantasy of achieving power and control didn't really happen, because they're not around to reap the fruits of their decision.

Suicide, Sexuality, and Secrets

"In all the teenage suicides we see," says Washington, D.C. counselor Judy Pollatsek, "the kids always have some secret and are terrified that someone is about to find out." Of course, all teenagers—and all people—have secrets. But a secret that would terrify a person into completing or attempting suicide is not just any secret. It's usually a secret that the teenager feels—rightly or wrongly—will threaten his or her entire world.

Often such secrets have to do with sex. That's because in our society, sexual standards and choices vary so much, even within a single community. What do you do if your parents think that sex before marriage is wrong—but all your friends seem to be having sex? What do you do if many of the people around you think that homosexuality is wrong, but you feel attracted to people of the same sex anyway? Teenagers must sort out their own feelings, the behavior of their friends, the beliefs of their parents, the teachings of their religion, and the standards of their community as they try to find their own way of dealing with physical relationships and sexual feelings.

Under these circumstances, if a girl gets pregnant, she may not just have a secret. She may have a secret that she believes—rightly or wrongly—will affect the way everyone she knows will think about her. Or she may think that her parents will be furious, or disappointed in her, or hurt, or a shamed, with a force that none of her other actions could bring on.

Of course, not all parents feel that way about a teenage pregnancy. But the importance that our society places on sex, along with the secrecy that usually surrounds it, may combine to make a pregnant teenager feel as if her secret is too terrible to bear. Under those circumstances, suicide might seem preferable to being found out. The girl may also feel that if she acts out her desperation and her fear by *attempting* suicide, her parents will focus on her needs rather than on her "crime" of getting pregnant.

Likewise, because so many people in our society are prejudiced against gay people, a boy or a girl who feels attracted to members of the same sex may feel that death is better than life "as an outcast." Boys are under a great deal of pressure to be "real men," which they often believe means not being "fairies" or "fags." Girls are under a lot of pressure to be "real women," which they may think means getting a boyfriend and valuing boys above girls.

The sad thing is that by killing themselves or attempting suicide, girls and boys are actually preventing themselves from finding out more about their sexual feelings. One of the most exciting challenges of adulthood—difficult though it may also be—is discovering the kind of relationships you want and the kind of sexual feelings that you bring to them. As with all the other situations we have described, suicide is no solution. It doesn't resolve difficult feelings. It doesn't bring peace, contentment, self-acceptance—or sexual satisfaction. It only takes all your feelings away from you—with no possibility of getting them back. (For more specific suggestions on coping with teenage sexual issues, see Chapter 4 and 6.)

Looking Deeper

In this chapter, we've examined the chain of events and thoughts that might lead a person to commit suicide. But we haven't explained why some people find this chain so compelling while others seem to be free of it. What makes a person feel vulnerable to suicidal thoughts? What distinguishes the small percentage of people who actually attempt or commit suicide from the vast majority of people who do not deal with stress, depression, or loss in this way?

Although no one really knows the answers to these questions, psychologists and sociologists have come up with some possible theories, which we'll explore in the next chapter.

3

The Deeper Reasons

So far, Maria has resisted hurting herself too badly with her razor blade. But now she feels like she's just numbing out. First Tony disappointed her, now Luce. It seems to Maria that she would just rather not feel anything at all because she only gets hurt.

If she's not feeling numb, she's feeling angry. Every little thing seems to get to her—her mother asking for help around the house, a teacher telling her when an assignment is due, the bus driver asking her to hurry up and move inside the bus. The only time Maria doesn't feel numb or angry is when she's been drinking or is high. Then she feels so happy and relaxed or very peaceful, as if the world is very far away and can't really touch her. When she's drunk or high, she pictures herself floating high above the rest of the world, safe inside her own little silver balloon, looking down below at everyone she knows, so high that no one can reach her at all.

As far as everyone else can tell, Charles is doing fine. No one even knows about his D on the chemistry test, especially since, by hard studying and doing extra work, he got a B for the semester. He and his girlfriend go out most Friday and Saturday nights, he hangs out with his buddies during the week, he continues to be helpful and pleasant at home with his family. His teachers all like Charles; he's the kind of student they can count on to come to class, do the work, and ask interesting questions.

That's why no one understands it when they hear about what Charles did. One Saturday night, after he dropped his girlfriend back at her house, Charles went out to the tree outside his parents' window and hanged himself. Fortunately, the noise he was making woke his parents, and they were able to rush outside in time to save him. But no one can understand what made Charles try to take his own life. Didn't he have everything?

Evie's favorite teacher is getting quite worried about her. Evie used to be a good student, but now she sits in the back row and seems to be daydreaming. The few times Evie's teacher has invited her out for coffee after school, Evie has made some excuse and drifted off. But when the teacher calls Evie's mother, the mother brushes her concern away. "I'm sure there's nothing wrong with my daughter," her mother says. "Teenagers are just like that."

Evie finds herself spending more and more time thinking about death. She writes poems about it, reads other people's poems about it, and thinks constantly about how peaceful and happy dead people must feel. She also finds herself planning just how she will kill herself when the time comes. She has been stealing one of her mother's sleeping pills each day, hiding the pills away in the back of her dresser. Sometimes after dinner, Evie goes up to her room, lights some candles, reads a poem about death aloud, and then takes out the pills and counts them over and over again. She writes in her journal, "The only thing I own is my life. The only way

I can be free is to give my life away." The only thing Evie doesn't yet know is when will be the right moment to take the pills. Meanwhile, she keeps collecting them.

People at Risk

As we saw in Chapter 2, most teenagers feel stressed out and depressed at least some of the time. And many teenagers find that adolescence is the unhappiest time of their life. But only a very few teenagers choose to commit or attempt suicide out of their unhappiness. What makes the difference? What kind of person is most at risk?

No one knows all the answers to that question. It really isn't possible to predict who will commit suicide and who will not. In fact, one expert calls suicide a "slot machine." Robert Litman, a psychologist at the Los Angeles Suicide Prevention Center, says that just as in a slot machine in which, say, three apples have to come up to hit a jackpot, so for suicides, there must be several "strikes" against someone to finally push the person to suicide. Litman says that we all start out with one, two, or three strikes against us. If you have a crisis in your life—your parents get a divorce, a close friend dies, you have a major problem in school—that might push you up to four strikes. If you have two crises, perhaps that's five. But to get six strikes—so many things going wrong at once—is as unusual as hitting the jackpot on a slot machine.

As you can see, this analogy focuses not on the personality of the suicide but on his or her circumstances. Litman is suggesting that given enough bad circumstances, anyone could consider taking his or her own life. He may also be explaining why teenagers have the lowest suicide rate of any adult age group—older people have had more time to have "bad things" accumulate.

Another approach to who is at risk is more statistical. When sociologists and psychologists analyze information about suicides and attempted suicides, what do they find?

Completers Versus Attempters

One of the most important distinctions in the research on suicide concerns the difference between people who attempt suicide but do not complete it and people who actually end their own lives. Although every suicide attempt is serious and significant, no matter what the outcome, many researchers believe that many people attempt suicide without ever intending to actually die. Instead, this group of "attempters" is using suicide to act out a truth about their lives, to dramatize how serious their problems are, to ask for help.

This insight is borne out by the statistics cited by George Howe Colt in *The Enigma of Suicide*. He points out that some 90 percent of all teenage suicide attempts are made at home, 70 percent of them while the parents are actually in the house. A person who attempts suicide under these conditions seems to want to be found and helped. Tragically, people who attempt suicide may be hurt too badly to be saved, no matter how carefully they have staged their attempt. Remember the story of the poet Sylvia Plath from Chapter 1; although Plath had carefully planned to be rescued after her suicide attempt, even leaving a note with her doctor's phone number on it, her plan misfired and she actually died.

Understanding the "attempters" is important if we are going to understand teenage suicide, since 120,000 adolescents do attempt suicide every year. And for every teenager who actually dies in a suicide, 20 have made the attempt.

Interestingly, this 20-to-1 ratio between teen attempters and those who actually die is much higher than the corresponding ratio for adults of approximately 3 or 4 to 1. (Only 1 to 2 percent of the population as a whole completes a suicide, compared with the 4 to 5 percent that attempts it.) This suggests that for most teenagers, suicide represents a wish for help or change more than for a wish for death.

Statistics show that three times as many women as men *attempt* suicide, but three times as many men as women *complete* suicide. Partly this is because men have traditionally chosen more violent and final ways of killing themselves—with guns, by hanging, by jumping from a high place. Women are more likely to use pills or to cut their wrists, methods that allow a person to be rescued or even to change her mind and ask for help. Of those in the total population who attempt suicide but continue to live, some 70 to 90 percent use pills and 10 percent cut their wrists, generally in settings that make it possible for them to survive. One suicide survivor remembers making a huge cut in her wrist, then calling out for her mother. When her mother did not respond, she staggered out of the bathroom and knocked on her mother's door, calling all the while.

What else do we know about that group of teenagers that attempts but does not complete suicide? Psychiatrist Barry Garfinkel studied 505 children and adolescents who had attempted suicide, comparing them with a control group of young people who had not attempted suicide. He found that the attempters came from what he called families in "disintegration"—families marked by medical problems, mental illness, alcohol and drug abuse, unemployment, and a rate of suicide or attempted suicide eight times higher than that of the other group.

Child psychiatrist Cynthia Pfeffer of Cornell University Medical College also found problems with the parents of suicidal children. According to her research, these parents were often subject to intense mood shifts, had a hard time waiting for what they wanted, and were often very dependent on their children. In other words, these parents were often like children themselves. Instead of being able to guide their children, they somehow expected their children to take care of them.

Harvard researcher Eva Deykin studied 159 adolescents who attempted suicide and found that they were often responding to physical or sexual abuse. Because of the violence their parents had shown toward them, she believed that they had learned to be violent in response to their problems—and then turned the violence on themselves.

Los Angeles Suicide Prevention Center psychiatrists also found a history of family violence in the suicidal teenagers they studied. Over 40 percent of them had had physical fights with their families, suggesting that violence and suicide are closely linked.

Both people who attempt and those who complete suicide seem to have suffered a serious loss at an early age. This pattern was first noted by Leonard M. Moss and Donald M. Hamilton. Their famous study of hospitalized attempted suicide patients in New York in the 1950s found that 95 percent of the people in the survey had undergone the death or dramatic and tragic loss of people related to them. And in 75 percent of the cases studied, the loss took place before adolescence. In other words, people who lost parents or close relatives at an early age seem to be especially vulnerable to suicide (though not necessarily to *teenage* suicide). This trend had been noted much earlier, in 1938, by psychiatrist Gregory Zilboorg, who noted a greater frequency of parental death in the histories of his suicidal patients.

A University of Washington study of 114 completed and 121 attempted suicides also found that if a person had lost a parent while still in childhood, he or she was significantly more likely to *complete* suicide rather than only to attempt it. (Again, this study was not limited to teenagers.) And if this parent had died from a suicide, then the person's own chances of completing suicide were significantly increased.

The Mourning Process

Why would losing a parent or loved one at an early age make a teenager or an adult wish for death? To approach this question, we have to understand the mourning process, the means by which people come to terms with loss and separation.

According to theories developed by Sigmund Freud and his follower Melanie Klein, when a person loses someone beloved, a mourning process begins. You feel the grief and pain of separation, and you wish intensely to be reunited with the lost love. These feelings apply whether the loss results from death, divorce, rejection, or simply growing apart. But since children need their parents or guardians more than any adult or teenager ever needs anyone, a child's loss of a parent is the most intense and the most difficult to accept.

If an adult or a teenager loses someone beloved, he or she may eventually be able to complete the mourning process. According to Freud, this happens as we identify with the person who has left us. In a sense, we "take that person into ourselves" by thinking of how we are like that person, by experiencing our feelings about him or her, by holding on to our memories and experiences of the person. Then, even though the person is gone, we have the sense that he or she lives inside of us. We can cope with loss and separation by reuniting with the person in our thoughts and feelings.

Of course, every loss brings with it anger and resentment as well as loving feelings. Virtually everyone who loses a beloved person feels angry at that person—even if he or she didn't leave voluntarily but by dying. It's hard for all of us to bear our angry feelings at the person who left or died, but if we have enough outer support and inner resources, we may be able to work through our anger and go on to "take the person inside us" through memories and good feelings.

Children, though, have a much more difficult time understanding what is happening during a loss or a death. And if the adults around them tell them not to be angry or upset, they may have an even more difficult time handling the angry parts of their feelings. Teenagers and adults may also have trouble with this aspect of their emotions. That's why it's so important to find people to talk to during a crisis, people who will accept and understand your feelings and allow you to work through your anger as well as your grief.

What do children do if they can't handle the anger they feel at a parent who "deserts" them by dying? Sometimes, when people don't want to feel "bad" feelings like anger, they imagine that someone *else* is feeling them, maybe even the person they are mad at. So instead of feeling how angry *they* are at the dead parent, children might decide that the dead parent is mad at *them*. That would explain why the person went away, and that also makes the child's own anger easier to handle. Adults and teenagers who have difficulty feeling their anger may go through a similar process.

In that case, if we picture the "lost" person as angry with us, when we take that person "inside" ourselves, we are taking in an angry person. In a way, all of our own anger at that person for leaving us turns into anger at ourselves. Rage that someone we loved has died becomes rage at ourselves for still being alive. Children are especially vulnerable to this process, but teenagers and adults are not immune. People of any age may feel guilty or upset at being left alive when someone they love has died or left them—it's all part of how they handle their own anger at losing a person they loved or cared about.

This helps explain why a loss may trigger a suicide, why a loss through death is even more potent as a suicide trigger, and why a loss through suicide is the most potent of all. In each case, our anger at the person who left us may be taken in and turned into anger against ourselves. And if we know the person left us "on purpose," if he or she chose to die rather than be with us, we may be so angry that we can only cope with it by saying "Maybe I also deserve to die."

People who have attempted suicide and been rescued often talk about feeling a split inside themselves. There is a part of them that feels compelled to kill themselves, and there is a part of them that really wants very much to live. According to Freud's and Klein's theories, the part of them that insists on killing is the part that is angry with the person who left them. The part that wants to live is all the rest of their feelings, struggling to survive and to move on.

Of course, consciously, we may understand that the person we loved who committed suicide wasn't really choosing to leave *us*. We may understand that the person was so tormented, or frightened, or confused that he or she thought there was no choice but to die. On a rational level, we may accept that the suicide was part of this person's problem and had nothing to do with us, just as, logically, we understand that a person who dies in an illness or accident could not help what happened.

But underneath, on an emotional level, we may still be angry, with both death and suicide. If you've ever seen a baby crying, you can understand how this works. Babies don't understand *why* they're not getting what they want. You can't explain that the bottle is coming any minute, or that as soon as you put down the books you're carrying you'll come over and change the diaper. Babies only understand two things: wanting and getting or wanting and not getting. On some level, we all still carry that simple way of looking at things inside of us. No matter how strong and grown up we get, there is still a little part of us that feels the way we did when we were babies.

The solution is not to try to wipe that "baby" part out, or ignore it, or bury it. The solution is to feel the feelings that go along with it—anger, rage, frustration, longing—so that the feelings can come to the surface alongside some of the more grown-up feelings that we also have. If we can accept our feelings of anger and longing, along with our feelings of love and our good memories, we can work through all of our feelings of love and loss—whether we're talking about losing a boyfriend or girlfriend, growing apart from a friend, or facing a death. Discovering all of our feelings means that we can choose which ones to act on and which ones simply to accept. It also means we don't have to turn our feelings against ourselves.

Families in Distress

Of course, the loss of a beloved family member does not guarantee suicidal feelings. And many teenagers may feel suicidal even if they have never lost a loved one through death, divorce, or abandonment. What pushes some people to turn their feelings of anger and disappointment against themselves in such a painful way?

Physical Abuse

If children come from families where they are physically abused, they may get two powerful and dangerous messages: that they are worthless or bad, and that violence is a helpful response to a problem. By physically abused, we mean any physical contact that leaves marks, bruises, or broken bones; hitting with fists, weapons, or objects; burns; violent shaking, strangling, or choking; or throwing someone downstairs or into a wall. We also mean particularly severe punishments, such as forcing someone to stand or sit in an uncomfortable position or a frightening place, tying someone up, depriving someone of food or sleep, or forcing a person to undergo a physical hardship as punishment.

A person who has been treated in this way may not recognize the treatment as abuse. The parents or guardians who perform it may present is as reasonable punishment, explaining in great detail why the child "deserved" or "provoked" the behavior. Or the child may interpret the action as the parent's "bad temper" or "justified anger." The parent may even apologize afterward.

Nevertheless, such behavior *is* abuse—that is, it goes beyond the bounds of acceptable punishment or loss of temper. No matter how the adult involved presents the behavior, the child is not responsible for it and should not have to put up with it.

Thousands of children, though, live in homes where they *do* put up with it. What message are they getting? In effect, their parents are treating them like property. The parents are giving the message that their feelings are all-important, that the child's feelings don't matter and have no impact on the situation. The parents may also be giving the message that the child is somehow bad, that it is the *child's* actions that are making the bad things happen. The child may receive the message that the parents hate him or her and may feel "instructed" to commit suicide.

If one parent is abusive and the other is not, this message may be reinforced. The nonabusive parent might tell the child, "That's just your mother's bad temper; don't take it seriously" instead of saying "How terrible that someone would treat you so badly! I'm going to put a stop to that right now!" Or the nonabusive parent might say, "What did you do to upset your father? If you behaved better, he wouldn't get so angry," instead of saying "However badly you be-haved, that's no excuse for *him* to act so badly. He's sup-posed to be the grown-up around here; I expect him to control himself!" Instead of feeling like a valuable person whom parents will care for and protect, the child ends up feeling like a bad or dangerous person whom parents will hurt and blame.

A child who is abused probably also feels very angry at the parents who act so badly. But because all children need to depend on their parents for food, shelter, and care, it's very scary to get mad at a parent. It's even more scary to get mad at a parent who might take your anger and use it as an excuse to hurt you some more. So physically abused chil-dren may feel that they have nowhere to turn the angry feelings—except on themselves.

Frequently, physically abused children and teenagers do go on to hurt themselves in lots of ways. They may develop eating disorders—stuffing themselves (compulsive eating, bingeing), or starving themselves (anorexia), or eating too much and then forcing themselves to throw up (bulimia). They may try to numb themselves with drugs or alcohol, a process that some experts have called "self-medication"— trying to make the pain go away, but hurting themselves more in the process. They might burn themselves with cigarettes to see if they can "take it," or engage in stunts and dares that put their lives at risk. It's almost as if they are saying "If *you*, my parents, didn't think I deserved to be safe and well, I may just have to agree with you. *Now* what do you think of the way you treated me?" Anger at their parents gets all mixed up with anger at themselves, and so they behave the way their parents do—they hurt themselves.

If you or someone you know is being physically abused, we urge you to get help immediately. Talk to another adult you trust, contact an agency, or call a hot line. (Information on resources for you is available in Chapter 6.) No one should have to put up with being physically abused—and suicide—a murder of oneself—is only one of the sad consequences of being treated this way.

Sexual Abuse

Other children come from homes where they are sexually abused. We define sexual abuse as any kind of sexual contact between adults and children, or between a person under 18 and another significantly older adult or child. Sexual abuse can include intercourse; contact through mouth, genitals, or anus (rear opening); "tongue" kissing or other invasive kissing; having someone expose sexual areas of the body to you or forcing you to expose yourself to them; being tickled, caressed, hugged, or played with in an uncomfortable way; hearing someone "talk dirty" or being asked to "talk dirty"; being spied on or openly watched while getting dressed, using the bathroom, or taking a bath, or being put in a position where you have to watch another person perform those activities. It can happen to either girls or boys, and it can come from either men or women. A child can be sexually abused by parents, relatives, stepparents, family friends, or strangers. All sexual abuse is painful and upsetting, but probably the most difficult to handle is abuse by a parent or guardian, since that is the person who is supposed to take care of you.

As with physical abuse, sexual abuse gives a powerful message to children: that they are the property of another person and that their own feelings, wishes, and actions have no power. All children have to struggle with the reality that their parents or guardians are bigger and stronger than they are, and that they are dependent on them for food, shelter, and care. Naturally, this gives adults a lot of power and makes children very vulnerable. In nonabusive homes, however, children are taught that their bodies and their rights will be respected even when they are too young to defend themselves.

In abusive homes, on the other hand, children learn that "might makes right" and that parents always win. Both physically and sexually abused children may feel that suicide is the only way left for them to assert control over their own bodies. Sadly, as we saw when we looked at false ideas and wishful thinking, it's a self-defeating kind of control, one that ends as soon as death begins.

Sexually abused children may have been given other difficult messages from both the abusive and the nonabusive parent. They may be made to feel that the parent's sexual abuse is somehow their fault, that they seduced the parent or "made" him or her do it by being so sexy and desirable. They may feel that their sexual feelings, their bodies, or their behavior is somehow "bad" because it brings out such bad actions in another person. Of course, this isn't true. But in an abusive situation, the truth may be hard to hold on to.

As with physically abused children, children who are sexually abused will do almost anything rather than blame their parents for what's happening. It's just too scary to accept that the person who is supposed to take care of you is actually hurting you. So sexually abused children may either deny that anything bad is happening or blame themselves. Then all of their anger against the abusive parent is turned against themselves, and, like physically abused children, they may develop eating disorders, drug and alcohol problems, self-wounding behavior, or, in some cases, suicidal thoughts and actions.

The sexually abused child may also feel that he or she is carrying a secret, from the world at large or from the rest of the family. As with the pregnant teenager or the young person who thinks he or she may be gay, the abused child may interpret this "secret" as a badge of shame and disgrace. It may seem better to die than to admit to the "crime" of being abused. Tragically and mistakenly, suicide may come to seem the only way to cleanse the shame or end the humiliation.

In fact, sexual abuse *is* a crime—but it is the crime of the abuser, not of the child or teenager. Sexual abuse is *never* the child's fault. If you or someone you know is being sexually abused, we urge you to get help. Call a hot line or an agency, or find a trusted adult to help you. (Some helpful resources are listed in Chapter 6.) As with physical abuse, no one should have to put up with sexual abuse—nor with the depression, the self-destructive behavior, or the suicidal feelings that may result from it.

Emotional Abuse

A more subtle but no less deadly form of abuse is known as emotional abuse. This may take many shapes, but the easiest to spot is the verbal equivalent of physical abuse—yelling, insults, put-downs, excessive teasing, and other ways of speaking and acting that undermine a person's sense of worth and value.

As with other abused children, a child who is treated this way is given the message that he or she doesn't count, that parents have the right to say anything they please while the child has no rights. It's as if the child was not allowed to put up any boundaries between himself or herself and the outside world, not allowed to say "This far and no farther." Children who have grown up this way also may feel that suicide is the only way to assert themselves, to say "This is *one* thing that I can do that you can't make fun of or put down, *one* thing that I can do to show you how I feel." Of course, even after such a painful and dramatic move as suicide, there's no guarantee that the parents won't continue to disrespect the child, to argue and insult and put him or her down even after death. And even if the suicide works, so what? The child is still not around afterward to enjoy the parent's new respect. Taking control of a life through suicide is self-defeating because after people have killed themselves, they're not there to experience any of the results of their actions.

"Happy Families"

So far, we've talked about fairly obvious family problems— physical, sexual, and emotional abuse. But what about the children of families that seem happy and loving? Why might these children and teenagers consider or attempt suicide?

These suicides may be especially mysterious. In some cases, a family may truly have offered its children love, care, concern, and respect—and still, the teenager decides, for whatever reason, that death is preferable to life, that committing or attempting suicide is the only way to express his or her pain, rage, or confusion.

In other cases, though, a family may only seem to have offered its children the kind of care and concern they need. While these families—like the more openly abusive families—may *also* love their children, they may be treating them in ways that convey difficult or dangerous messages, ways that help convince the child that suicide is the only way out.

Mixed Messages

In Charles's family, people often *tell* each other how much they care. What they *show*, however, is something else.

For example, when Charles was little and he ran to hug his mother or father, they would almost always push him away. His father would say, "You're a big boy, you don't need to do that now. I'm so proud of my big boy!" His mother would say, "Isn't he sweet—he really loves his mother," while pushing Charles away at arm's length, as if to show him off. Both of Charles's parents were using words to say they loved him—but their actions were telling him something completely different. Both parents were actually pushing him away, refusing to take his affection or to offer him theirs.

Likewise, when Charles's debate team gave a special evening program, Charles's father said he couldn't come because he had to work late. "I know you'll understand— you're very mature for your age," his father told him. "I can't believe how grown up you are. I'm really proud of you." Charles's father was *saying* that he was proud of Charles, but at the same time, he was refusing to share his son's accomplishments, to take part in something that helped Charles be proud of himself. Charles's mother did go to the event, but afterward, when Charles asked her what she thought, she said, "Oh, you know I'm too dumb to keep up with all your big ideas. I just sat there and watched my boy." Although her words seemed to be compliments, the message Charles really got was "Oh, you think you're smarter than me, don't you?" Like his father, Charles's mother had refused to participate in his life and share his enjoyment of his successes. Somehow, what should have been a special evening for Charles was spoiled by his father's lack of caring and his mother's envy.

How does Charles react to all this? Deep down, he knows that something is wrong. He doesn't *feel* loved by his parents. He feels that his father doesn't want to be bothered by him, and his mother either wants to show him off or feels envious and resentful. But Charles knows he isn't "supposed" to have these feelings. He's supposed to think that he comes from a happy family that loves him very much. If he ever told his father he was angry or disappointed, his father would act hurt, angry, or upset with Charles. If he told his mother his true feelings, she too would be angry.

Like the abused children we discussed earlier, Charles doesn't want his parents to be wrong. He wants them to be wise and good, so that they can take care of him and offer him the help and guidance that he needs. So Charles will do anything to go along with his parents' image of themselves as good, loving parents.

Since deep down he knows this isn't true, however, Charles has an empty feeling inside. And since he's lying to himself about his parents, he has a hard time believing himself about *any* of his feelings. Maybe his girlfriend doesn't really love him either—how could he tell? Maybe his friends hang out with him only because he's cool, not because they really care. Maybe he's fooled his teachers into thinking he's smart, the way his parents have fooled *him* into thinking they're good parents. Because there is a big lie in his family, Charles feels like a fraud.

That's why a failure or setback, like his D in chemistry, makes Charles feel as if his whole world is unraveling. He knows that there's an unpleasant truth down there under all those lies—and when something bad happens, it feels very big, as if it's connected to that truth. Of course, the unpleasant truth is not about Charles, it's about his parents—that they are not providing him with the love and support he needs. But as we've seen before, Charles is turning his anger and disappointment about his parents against himself—even to the point of trying to kill himself.

Dependence and Independence

As we saw in Chapter 2, the teenage years can be difficult ones: Young people are still dependent on their parents, even as they seek their own independence. This can be a tricky struggle in any family, but some families make it even harder than it needs to be.

Some parents enjoy feeling that their children are dependent on them. Perhaps these parents feel inadequate or inferior in the world at large—so they need the love and admiration of their children to feel okay about themselves. They encourage their children to need them, even when their children might be able to become more independent.

When Charles picks out a shirt he likes, for example, his mother might say, "Oh, that looks terrible! Let me find you something nicer." Charles gets the message that he is not capable of picking out his own clothes, that he needs his mother to do it for him. Charles is being encouraged to stay more dependent than he needs to.

Other parents have a difficult time meeting their children's needs. They may encourage their children to do more for themselves than is appropriate to their age.

Maria's mother, for example, feels overwhelmed with all of the work she has to do running the household, earning a living, and caring for Maria and her six brothers and sisters. From a very young age she expected Maria, the oldest, to act like a "little mother" to her younger siblings. Maria didn't really get a chance to be a child herself because she was so busy taking care of other people.

Sometimes the same parents can expect their children to be both dependent and independent, according to how the parent feels that day. If these parents are feeling good and strong, they may enjoy having a child's needs to fulfill. If they are feeling needy and weak, they may want the child to act like a parent. In fact, they may want their children to take care of *them*.

Evie's mother, for example, often felt lonely and sad when her husband would withdraw into his depression. Sometimes she would cheer herself up by taking care of Evie. She would encourage her daughter to bring her problems to her, so that she could solve them. Solving Evie's problems made her mother feel strong and secure and helped her forget that she was unhappy with Evie's father.

Other times, Evie's mother felt like a child herself. Why couldn't she get her husband to feel better? Why didn't he want to come out of their room and spend time with her? In those moods, she turned to her daughter for companionship. Evie got the message that when her mother was unhappy, it was Evie's responsibility to cheer her up. In a mood like that, if Evie's mother asked her daughter to go shopping, Evie would feel too guilty to say no. She would think that her mother would be too lonely and unhappy if she, Evie, didn't take care of her. It was almost as if Evie felt like the mother and her mother felt like the daughter.

Children from families like this often have a difficult time coping with loss, failure, and disappointment because they haven't been given realistic feedback about what they can and can't do. They may be told that they're weaker than they really are, stronger than they really are, or both. In this climate, any disappointment or upset can seem unbearably confusing and upsetting. And of course, children like these are angry at their parents for not giving them the help and guidance that they have a right to expect. As we've seen before, this anger may get turned against themselves, as depression, self-destructive behavior, or even suicide.

Buried Feelings

Sometimes children have the strong feeling that their parents actually want them dead. This may take an open form, as in openly abusive families. Parents may actually say to children "You're nothing, you're worthless, you'd be better off dead," or "I can't stand the sight of you. I wish you were dead." Or they may tell stories about how they tried to have an abortion to prevent the child's birth, or tell other stories that carry the message that the child is a burden, a problem, or in the way.

In families that appear happier or more loving, children may still be getting deadly messages from their parents. Some parents have a lot of difficulty admitting their own feelings. They may indeed wish that they had never had children. Maybe they never really wanted to be parents. Maybe they never had the chance to think about it. Maybe parenthood turned out to be more difficult or more demanding than they thought. Of course, none of this is the child's fault. Children don't ask to be born—parents choose to have them. But if parents feel that their children "should not" exist, they may convey that message in subtle ways, even if they never say or think such a thing directly.

Children from families like this feel unwanted a great deal of the time. They try to please their parents by making themselves "not there." Often they have difficulty knowing what they feel or being in touch with their emotions. These children may feel so guilty about "disobeying" their parents that when they have strong feelings that make them feel alive—love, anger, excitement, even sadness—they also feel guilty, as if simply being alive and having feelings were hurting their parents. Children from such families may feel compelled to kill themselves when they start having powerful and "alive" feelings. They may even feel that their parents have "instructed" them to do so.

"Shadow Suicides": Self-Destructive Behavior

As we've mentioned, sometimes people who don't actually plan to commit suicide nevertheless act in ways that put their lives in danger. Drug and alcohol abuse, overeating, self-starvation, bulimia, smoking, reckless driving, stunts and dares, promiscuity and sexual risk-taking, and similar foolhardy actions may lead to injury or loss of life. While some people who do some of these things are otherwise quite careful of their health, others may seem to be trying to die without actually taking responsibility for choosing death.

Although they might never leave a suicide note, their behavior might be considered suicidal.

Ironically, the other side of reckless or dangerous behavior may be the wish to "wake up" feelings. Many suicidal teenagers report that they hate feeling numb and dead inside. Their suicide attempts—or their risky, self-destructive behavior—may have been ways to force themselves to feel *something*, even if what they finally feel is pain or terror.

One of the most common kinds of "accidental suicide" among teenagers is reckless driving. Although no one can ever be sure whether a death in a car accident was "accidental" or "accidentally on purpose," it does seem as if many teenagers (as well as many adults) get into accidents that suggest a wish to die or, perhaps more accurately, a wish to escape their lives.

Psychologists have spoken of certain uses of drugs and alcohol as being a kind of "self-modification," taken to numb feelings of pain, anger, or guilt that might otherwise seem unbearable. Maria's drug and alcohol use fits into that category. She is so afraid of her angry and painful feelings that she will do anything to shut them down. Someday, if drugs or alcohol doesn't work, she may finally turn to an actual suicide attempt.

Sometimes, too, a person who actually goes through with a suicide attempt will have "tried out" self-destruction in one of these other forms first. The person may be "practicing" behavior whose message is "I don't care whether I live or die," "Life is awful, anyway," or "I can't feel anything except pain—so let me at least feel that."

Deadly Thoughts

How does the world look to someone considering suicide? Here are some thoughts and feelings that suicidal people have had:

- "I don't deserve to live."
- "I'd rather feel pain than feel nothing."
- "I'm so angry I can't stand it."
- "I hate everything so much—I just want to destroy everything."
- "I just want the pain to stop."
- "I just want it all to be over."
- "My parents want me dead."
- "I'm programmed to be dead."
- "My feelings scare me."
- "I'm not supposed to feel this way."
- "There must be something wrong with me."
- "I'm so different from everybody else."
- "Why am I so lonely?"
- "It will never get any better."
- "I'm such a failure."
- "Nobody cares if I live or die."
- "The world is so messed up—it doesn't make sense."
- "It's not my world and it will never help me."
- "Nobody knows who I am."
- "Nobody really cares about me."
- "I'm so lonely I could die."
- "I just want to cut myself open and let all the bad things out."

If you've ever felt this way, you should know that you're not alone. In fact, most teenagers have probably thought at least some of those things at least once in their lives, and many people have felt some of those ways a lot of the time.

Just knowing that you're not alone in your unhappiness can help sometimes. But a teenager who is thinking about suicide often feels too lonely, too different, and too "bad" to break out of his or her isolation.

Evie often feels this way. She thinks—with some truth—that she is quite different from most of the kids at her high school, who don't seem to like poetry and books the way she does. She also thinks—with a lot less truth—that there is nobody in the whole world who is like her. She cannot imagine a future in which she leaves home, goes out into the world, and makes friends like her. She cannot imagine a way to be herself and to find a place in the world. Because she cannot imagine a future or a world outside the one she knows, her deadly thoughts have all the power.

"Happy All the Time"

Part of the pressure on teenagers in our society is the idea that somehow, we're all supposed to be happy all the time. "If you have a problem, you should solve it!" "If you're feeling bad, it's your fault!" "If you're poor or in a bad situation, pull yourself up by your bootstraps!" Sound familiar? There may be something optimistic and empowering about a philosophy of "positive thinking," a philosophy that stresses self-help and self-reliance, but there can also be something quite cruel about it. It may leave no room for a teenager's loneliness, confusion, or frustration. It may also make difficult articulating and confronting problems that are quite real—poverty, racism, poor schools, bureaucratic attitudes, a hollow emphasis on material wealth, pollution, the nuclear danger.

If you are concerned with problems in yourself, your family, and your world, take heart. Not only are you not alone, you are doing the work that a teenager is supposed to do—figuring out your identity and your place in the world. You may take your new knowledge and make a new contribution—a poem, a scientific invention, a special kind of business. Or you may want to change the world you've been born into, to fight against the problems you see and nurture new ways of organizing society. Meanwhile, you may feel frustrated because those opportunities seem far in the future of adulthood, and you are still only a teenager.

The way through the painful and deadly feelings we recorded is not to numb them out with drugs or alcohol or to bury them under a cheerful facade. The way through them is to feel the feelings—and to break out of isolation, to find people who can appreciate and respect you while you work toward a future in which you have more power and freedom than you do now. In the next chapter, we'll suggest some ways for getting help with deadly thoughts and suicidal feelings.

4

Breaking the Cycle: Getting Help

One night Maria goes riding with some drinking buddies when they're all pretty high. The car gets into a terrible crash in which the driver is killed. Maria is really shaken up by this. She was with the friend when he died in the smashed-up car, and she finally saw death at close quarters. She realizes that she really doesn't want to die—and that the way things are going, she will die soon unless she gets help.

Maria finds out about a local chapter of Alcoholics Anonymous (AA) that has a special support group for teenagers. Going to the meetings and talking with other people who share her problems seem to help. There are still times, however, when she wants to get out her razor blade and cut herself, and she's starting to wonder whether she should be getting another kind of help as well.

When Charles's family took him to the emergency room after he hanged himself, they were given the numbers of a family therapist and a suicide support group. After they took

Charles home, they threw the numbers away. "It was just a silly misunderstanding," his mother says. "We're perfectly able to work out our problems by ourselves." She makes sure that Charles goes to school as usual the next day, so that the neighbors don't talk.

Charles seems to be getting better. He tells everyone who knows about what happened not to worry. He even jokes about it with his friends. Some of them are pretty impressed by the marks on Charles's neck, as if it took a special kind of courage to do what he did. His girlfriend is still worried about him, but Charles insists that nothing's wrong. Then, a few months later, he disappears. When his family finally calls the police, Charles's body is discovered—hanging from a tree in the farthest corner of the community park. This time, Charles made sure he wouldn't be found.

Late one night, Evie finally gathers up her courage and takes the dozen sleeping pills she's been saving. Then, immediately, she wonders why she did it. She knocks on the door of her mother's bedroom and says, "I just thought I'd tell you, I took a bunch of pills." Instantly her sleepy mother wakes up and bombards her with questions. "What kind of pills? How many? When did you take them?" It's almost as if she's been expecting this. She bundles Evie into the car and rushes her to the emergency room.

The doctors at the hospital give Evie ipecac to make her throw up. It smells terrible and she feels awful for hours afterward. As soon as she feels even a little bit better, her mother starts in on her. "How could you do this to me? Do you have any idea what you put us through? What were you thinking?" When things finally calm down, she tells Evie that she's going take her to see a counselor. "Maybe she'll straighten you out," Evie's mother says.

But actually, the counselor wants to talk to both of them. Gradually both Evie and her mother start talking about their real feelings. Evie's mother talks about how lonely she feels, and how sometimes she doesn't know whom to take care of first—Evie or herself. Evie talks about how angry she feels with both her parents. Why does her mother need her so much? Why couldn't her father pay more attention to her when he was alive?

It doesn't happen right away. But gradually, little by little, Evie starts to feel better. At least now she and her mother are talking. At least now somebody notices what's really going on with her.

Overcoming Isolation

The deadliest feeling in the world may be the sense of isolation. Sometimes it seems as if human beings can stand anything—as long as they're in it together. That may be why the worst punishment in prison is solitary confinement. Shutting a person up by himself or herself, with no one to talk to or share things with, may be the cruelest punishment of all.

Suicidal feelings feed on isolation. When you're all alone, it's easy to feel that nobody else has ever felt the way you do. When you're not talking with anyone, it's easy to feel that you are different or weird. When you're not sharing your true feelings with people you care about it, it's easy to feel that they don't know or love the real you, and to wonder whether they would like you if they knew you.

Often people attempt suicide because they have become so isolated, they can't think of any other way of reaching out. Isolation may be especially intense if a person lives in a family that likes to pretend nothing is wrong. Families that insist on everyone being "happy all the time" may increase a teenager's sense of isolation if he or she is *not* happy. And of course, it's not possible to be happy *all* the time, especially if you're a teenager! Yet if no one in a family is acknowledging the unhappiness, the teenager may feel increasingly isolated and cut off. He or she may feel that committing or attempting suicide is the only way to say "Things are *not* okay!"

Teenagers often talk about "saving" their true selves for the people who can understand and appreciate them. Often, in all kinds of families, teenagers don't feel that their parents can be those people. That's part of growing up—figuring out your parents' limits and finding other people outside the family to bond with. But if you feel that *nobody* notices that you are not being your true self, neither your parents nor your friends, the isolation may become too painful to bear.

What's the answer? It sounds so simple but it can be so hard to do—reach out. Find someone to talk to. Seek out people with whom you can be your true self. If you don't get along with your parents, maybe there's an aunt or an uncle whom you can talk to, or a teacher, or a janitor, or a clerk in the neighborhood store. If you don't like the people in your classes, what about people at school with different schedules, or people doing different activities from the ones you've tried? Or what about people in your community—at the Y or local sports teams, or in the community theater?

Teenagers who are concerned about being gay might want to reach out to gay community groups, so that they can explore the truth of who they are and decide for themselves what relationships they want and what lifestyle they feel drawn to. Likewise, teenagers who are worried about being pregnant might look for community groups or agencies that can help them make the best decisions for themselves and offer them the resources to back up their decisions.

If you really feel that there's no one in your family, your school, or your community with whom you can be yourself, don't give up. Remember that many people have felt that way, and they found a solution—when they got old enough, they moved. Start figuring out where you'd like to live when you get older. Research the places where you'd like to go to college, or the city you'd like to live in when you turn 18. Find out what kind of jobs you can get, read books about other people who have lived there, even buy street maps and start learning the neighborhoods that you'd like to explore. The important thing is to remember that there is a world in both space and time beyond the one you're living in. Find a way to reach out to the life you want.

Meanwhile, or course, you can keep looking for someone to talk to where you are. You may find it easier to reach out in your own time and place once you know that you don't have to stay there forever.

Accepting Your Feelings

Another helpful thing you can do for yourself is to accept your feelings, whatever they may be. That doesn't mean acting on them, or even believing that they are "real." If you feel like the loneliest person in the world, that doesn't mean you *are* the loneliest person in the world. But your loneliness is real—that's your genuine feeling. If you feel so bad and worthless that you think you'd like to die, that doesn't mean you should kill yourself. It means accepting that you feel very bad right now, that something isn't working well in your life as it is.

An adult woman who remembers her two teenage suicide attempts says that she'd like to tell all teenagers "You are a person, and even your most insane feelings come from somewhere." *Acting* on those insane feelings may not be a good idea. But *recognizing* the feelings and trying to understand the message that they're giving you is the first step toward changing your life in ways that work for you.

Sadly, parents and families often minimize a teenager's feelings. Even after a teen attempts suicide, parents might continue to ignore the seriousness of the problem. In one study cited by George Howe Colt in *The Enigma of Suicide*, only 38 percent of the families involved acted on referrals that they were given after their teenagers attempted to kill themselves. And another study found that only 41 percent of the families of attempted suicides went for further therapy. If this is how deeply these families denied their children's feelings even *after* a suicide attempt, imagine how the children's feelings were ignored before.

If a teenager's suicide attempts are belittled or ignored, the teen may feel compelled to do more. Colt describes a teenage girl who slashed her wrists and then came down to breakfast every day with her sleeves rolled up, revealing the scars. No one in her family noticed—or at least, no one commented. Eventually she felt forced to make a more serious attempt.

According to statistics Colt cites, 10 percent of those who attempt suicide once will do it again, 2 percent within the same year. And 25 to 40 percent of those who actually complete a suicide have made a previous attempt.

John Tiebout, a counselor at the Suicide Crisis and Center in Dallas, sees teenage suicide as an attempt to communicate. "Today teenagers have to go to more and more extremes to get what they want. And maybe suicide fits into that dynamic," he says. "Being depressed or getting high is not a strong enough way to communicate to the world how miserable and screwed up you are."

The woman remembering her teen suicide attempts agrees. "I wish somebody had noticed I was really screwed up," she says. Since nobody did, she felt driven to dramatize her situation by taking several pills. Three years later, she slashed her wrist. Fortunately, she recovered from both attempts. "I never intended to die," she says. But she looks back with gratitude and relief, knowing that she took an enormous chance.

Breaking the Barriers

A suicidal teenager might seek help from friends, family, new acquaintances, support groups, therapists and counselors, or some combination of these. But in order to seek help, he or she must be ready to reach out. Ironically, the very things that drove a person to attempt suicide may be the things that make it difficult to seek or accept help.

Here are some reasons that people keep from seeking or accepting the help they need:

- They think that accepting help makes you weak.
- They think that accepting help means you're a failure.
- They've been so disappointed in the past by parents, friends, or others, they can't bear to trust anyone ever again.
- They don't believe anyone is capable of giving them help.
- They fear that the helper will take advantage of their weakness and try to control or manipulate them.
- They feel that if they talk honestly about their problems, they will be betraying their families.
- They feel guilty for going outside their families for any-thing—if the family can't provide it, they shouldn't need it.
- They feel that if they're having problems, it must mean they've done something wrong, and they deserve the pain.
- They feel ashamed to admit how badly off they are.

These are some of the feelings that might keep a person from getting help. On the other hand, consider what happens if a person does *not* get help. In all probability, things will not get better. In fact, they might get worse. The pain that led to the first suicide attempt won't go away if nothing else changes. Neither will the anger, or the guilt, or the numbness, or the sense of being out of control.

On the other hand, consider what might happen if a person does get help. He or she has a chance to work through feelings that have been painful and difficult to handle for a long time. There's an opportunity to fix what-ever isn't working, to open up new options, to take positive action to build a new life. Many people who were unhappy enough to attempt suicide have gone on to become happy adults with satisfying, rewarding lives. Taking that first step to reach out may be painful—but it's a pain that can bring relief and, eventually, even joy.

Kinds of Help

Therapy

People of all ages and with all kinds of problems often find that some kind of formal therapy or counseling is helpful. A trained therapist can help you accept and feel all of your feelings, as well as help you to sort through which feelings are based in reality and which are based in distorted ideas that may not be true.

A trained therapist may be a social worker, a psychologist, a psychiatric nurse, or a psychiatrist. A suicidal teen will probably find it helpful to see someone with special training in dealing with suicide. Although therapy can be expensive, it is often available for free or at low cost from city or state agencies.

Talking about your feelings with a therapist can be a painful as well as a liberating experience. People often find that in the beginning stages of therapy, they experience enormous relief at finally having someone to talk to. They may also discover that feelings of anger, shame, guilt, or sorrow are coming up more strongly than ever. That's because these feelings may have been buried before. As buried feelings, they worked their way into suicidal or self-destructive behavior. But as these feelings are expressed openly, they can be challenged and examined, so that they no longer rule a person's life.

One of the things a trained therapist can help with is letting go of guilt, shame, and self-blame. A therapist can help people understand and accept their feelings, so that they can love and accept themselves.

Support Groups and Group Therapy

Many teenagers find it helpful to join support groups of others who have attempted or considered suicide. Such groups are usually led by a trained professional who helps each group member work through and share his or her feelings.

Group therapy has many of the same advantages as individual therapy, along with the chance to share experiences with other people who have "been there" too. Many people do both group and individual therapy, especially during times of crisis.

Family Therapy

Sometimes the most effective type of therapy involves not just the teenager but the entire family. Some family therapists see family members separately as well as together. Some focus on the parents; others include brothers and sisters as well. The goal of family therapy is to help change family relationships to make them more satisfying for all. Presumably, a teenager who considers or attempts suicide is not getting the help and support he or she needs from the family. Probably other family members are also experiencing problems of some kind, which keep them from recognizing and responding to the teenager's needs. Family therapy gives everybody a chance to get his or her feelings out into the open and provides perspective on how family members might better approach their problems and their relationships.

Hot Lines

For the teenager who feels drawn to suicide or self-destructive behavior, a suicide hot line may be a good first step. Most hot lines are anonymous—that is, a teenager can talk to someone without having to give a name or any identification, although counselors may ask for a name if they believe a person is about to kill himself or herself. Ideally, a hot line counselor will let a suicidal person know that he or she is not alone and will suggest places to go for further help. For more information on hot lines, see Chapter 6.

Making Connections

Suicide is a difficult and painful problem, and no one should have to face it alone. As teenagers cope with their suicidal and self-destructive feelings, they are also taking positive steps to re-create their lives. In the end, the best response to a teen's attempted suicide may be to understand it as a message, a sign that something is terribly wrong. On the one hand, that message brings pain and fear, as the suicidal person recognizes just how bad things have gotten. On the other hand, that message may bring hope and promise, as the person looks ahead to make new choices and new connections.

Overcoming isolation is a two-way street, however. What about the family and friends of the suicidal person? How do they cope with *their* responses to this painful act? We'll discuss that side of the connection in the next chapter.

5

Reaching Out: Coping with the Suicidal Feelings of Another

Now that things are going better for her, Maria has gotten closer to her friend Luce. But sometimes, being Maria's friend is hard for Luce. Maria is still often depressed, angry, and upset about her life, even though she is working through these feelings in AA and in therapy. Since Maria has stopped drinking and using drugs, she's not always as much fun to be with—she can be more serious and more intense than before. Maria has explained to Luce that she's going through a lot of changes, and that other people in AA have told her that the first year after you stop drinking and using drugs is often hard. That's because all sorts of new feelings come up that the drinking and drugs were helping you to bury. Luce understands—but it's still tough on her sometimes. She wants to be supportive of Maria—but she doesn't want to get swallowed up in her friend's problems or feelings.

Charles's family was devastated after Charles died. His parents were in shock for a few weeks, and his younger sisters felt terrible. Not only had they lost their brother, but it seemed that they had "lost" their parents too. The parents were so absorbed in their grief about Charles that they were ignoring their other chldren.

Charles's girlfriend also felt guilty and upset. She wished that she had paid attention to her own instincts and made Charles talk more about what was going on with him. She felt that if she really loved Charles, she would have known how serious his problems were. She thought that somehow, she should have been able to help him. And she was angry with Charles for hurting himself that way. Besides all the guilt and anger, she missed someone she cared about, and she felt very sad about continuing her life without him.

As Evie and her mother continue to see their family counselor, their relationship has its ups and downs. Some days Evie even misses the old ways, when no one talked honestly with anybody else and she didn't feel anything except her own "blahs." There are days when she feels overwhelmed by her feelings plus those of her mother.

On other days, though, Evie feels closer to her mother than she ever has. And she feels freer. She understands that her father's depression was his problem, not hers. She realizes that sometimes it's all right to say no to her needy mother. And she's starting to make a couple of friends at school, other kids who like poetry and serious discussions. She hasn't quite figured out how honest to be with these new friends—should she tell them about her suicide attempt, or would that give them the wrong idea? Just as she is learning how to be more open about her feelings with her family, though, she is finding new ways to connect to these friends too.

Danger Signals

Suicide almost never happens "out of the blue." In four out of five cases, the suicidal person gives several warning signals indicating what he or she is planning. Sometimes these warning signs are noticeable only in hindsight. Sometimes, though, they are more obvious, because the suicidal person is really hoping that someone will notice what is going on and offer help.

Remember when we talked about suicidal people feeling split? Part of them wants to die, but part of them wants to live. As Erwin Stengel, author of *Suicide and Attempted Suicide*, puts it, "Most people who commit suicidal acts do not either want to die or to live. They want to do both at the same time, usually the one more, or much more, than the other."

You might think of the part of the person that wants to live as a prisoner deep down inside a dungeon. All around the prisoner are strong defenses—all the things that the person does to keep you and other caring people away. Drugs and alcohol might be defenses, or violent behavior, or insults. Or perhaps the person's defenses take the form of being quiet and withdrawn, of seeming not to care about anything—or even of acting happy and content, of denying that anything is even wrong.

Yet way down behind those defenses, the prisoner—the part of the person that wants to live—is trying to get through. He or she is sending messages—clues, warning signs—that something is terribly wrong, that he or she is in danger. Even though the defenses are sending out the message that everything is fine, the prisoner is sending out a message of "Help me! Notice me! Don't listen when the rest of me says I'm okay! Don't listen when the rest of me tells you to mind your own business!"

What are the warning signs that the "prisoner" might be sending out? Some of them may look like this:

Possible Warning Signs of Suicide

- **Giving away possessions** "I won't be needing this any more," the person might say, or, "I always wanted you to have this."
- **Making negative remarks about the future** Remarks like "The world is better off without me" or "Nothing is every going to work out for me" are often hints of a person's state of mind.
- **Talking about the future as if the person won't be there** "You won't be seeing me around any more" or "Too bad I won't be around to see it" might be clues that a person is planning a suicide.
- **Preoccupation with death, dying, or what happens after death** Of course, many teenagers are interested in death, in religion, and in the idea of an afterlife. But if a person seems to think about these topics all the time, or to be particularly attracted to the afterlife, or to portray death as calm or peaceful or the solution to life, that person might be sending you a signal.
- **Signs of severe depression** As we saw in Chapter 2, these signs include changes in appearance; altered eating or sleeping habits; problems in school; difficulty concentrating; lethargy and fatigue; loss of interest in friends; lack of pleasure in previously enjoyed activities; expressions of worthlessness and self-hate; excessive risk-taking; problems with drugs and alcohol; and preoccupation with death, dying, or suicide.

How to Respond

What do you do if someone you know is showing one or more of these signs? What if none of the signs seems to be present but you just have a funny feeling about someone? How do you handle it?

The first thing to do is to bring up the subject. Ask "Are you serious?" Or say "It sounds like you're talking about suicide. Are you?" As we pointed out in Chapter 1, talking about suicide with someone who is thinking about it won't make the person any more suicidal. In fact, having the chance to talk about it might be a relief.

Many people don't want to bring up the topic of suicide because they're afraid the person will be offended or angry. The person might be—but isn't it better to take the chance than to find out later that he or she really was planning a suicide? You might say something like "When I hear you talk like that, I get worried. It sounds like you're planning to hurt yourself, or to kill yourself. Are you?"

What do you do if the person says yes? Experts suggest that you start by saying "Please don't." Sometimes that's all it takes.

It might also be a good idea to ask the person if he or she has a specific plan. It's important to take seriously anyone who talks about suicide, but a person who has made a plan is in far more danger. The more specific the plan, the more likely that the person plans to use it. At that point, you might say "Let's go get help." If the person seems to be ready to act on the plan, stay with him or her and don't leave until you can get the help of an adult you trust. If you can't think of anyone else to call, try a suicide hot line and ask to be referred to somebody.

Sometimes a person considering suicide just needs to talk. Hearing a person talk about the anger, despair, or loneliness that makes suicide seem like a good option might be upsetting or scary, but if you can handle it, it may be a great kind of help to offer. In such a case, you might work on being what some psychologists call "an active listener." Here are the rules for active listening, used by many counselors at suicide hot lines:

- **Don't argue or contradict** Allow the person to express his or her feelings, whatever they may be. If the person says "Everything in my life is terrible," it won't help for you to say "But you have so much to live for." The person already knows that he or she "shouldn't" be feeling so awful—that hasn't changed the feeling. Your saying that the feelings don't make sense will only make the person feel more guilty and inadequate.

- **Don't express shock or disapproval** Again, saying something like "How can you feel that way?" or "But suicide is a sin!" will probably only make the person feel worse. No one chooses suicide because they think it's a good idea—they choose it because they feel they have no other choice. They are already more upset that they feel this way than you are, even if they are acting calm and secure.

- **Do encourage the person to express all of his or her feelings** If the person slows down or stops, you might allow a silence to go on for a while, to see if he or she has anything more to say. If not, you might repeat the last thing the person said in your own words, to convey that you're listening and you're interested in any feeling the person wants to express. If, for example, the person says "Sometimes I just can't stand my parents!" you might say "So you don't like your parents sometimes?" or "Boy, you sound like you're really mad at your folks." You might also ask why he or she feels that way.

- **Express your own feelings** Telling the person that you care is helpful. It might also help to say how sad it makes you to hear that the person is feeling so bad.

- **Take the person seriously** Sometimes people who are thinking of suicide feel the need to laugh and joke and pretend that nothing's wrong, even while they are talking about ending their own lives. Talking about suicide is the message from the "prisoner"; laughing and joking are the defenses that are supposed to distract you from the message. Sometimes even a person who has already attempted suicide will try to make a joke of it, or will brag and show off the scars. Deep down, that person wants someone to hear his or her pain, but it may feel safer not to admit this, in case no one responds. Of course, sometimes joking is a good way to deal with a difficult situation. But make sure you let your friend know that you take seriously the pain that he or she is in. And make sure that joking doesn't interfere with your friend getting the help that he or she needs.

If you know or suspect that a friend or acquaintance is thinking about suicide, we urge you not to handle this problem alone. Tell your parents, your friend's parents, a sympathetic teacher or counselor, or an adult you trust. If you can't think of anyone you know that you'd like to confide in, *you* call a suicide hot line, and tell them about the situation with your friend. You should not have to bear the burden of being the only person who knows about your friend's problem. If you can't convince your friend to get help, get help for yourself!

Dealing with Depression

What if you have a friend, a relative, or a classmate who is depressed, abused, or constantly angry? You can see how much this person needs support; you can see the link between these feelings and possible suicidal behavior. You care about this person, and you'd like to help. But you are also getting really tired of it all! After all, you have problems too. What do you do?

Like Maria's friend Luce, you are walking a fine line. On the one hand, you want to offer support; on the other hand, you want to take care of yourself. The first thing to remember is that you're having a hard time for a reason. It *is* difficult staying close to someone who is depressed; that's part of why depression is such a painful condition—because it keeps the depressed person isolated.

Here are some other suggestions for dealing with a depressed friend or relative:

- **Insist on making contact, even as you respect the person's privacy** A depressed person is likely to push you away, either by getting mad at you or by withdrawing. Perhaps this will make *you* mad in return. It's all right to feel that way—and it's all right, even helpful, to express that anger to the depressed person. Just make sure you *do* express it, rather than withdrawing yourself. For example, you might say "It really makes me mad when you shut me out," or "It's important to *me* to spend time with you, and I hate it when you act like you don't care." You might also say "It's okay if you're in a bad mood; I just want to spend some time with you. You don't have to be any special way."

- **Remember that the person's depression is his or her problem, not yours** It can be hard not to take someone's depression personally. It's easy to feel that a depressed person is rejecting *you*, that you have some-how failed. Take a closer look. Are you the only person that the depressed person is pushing away? Is he or she keeping around the friends who aren't so close, while pushing away the people who are closer? Try to see whether it is really *you* the person is reacting to, or whether he or she merely is acting out of his or her own feelings.

  Again, it's all right to get angry with a depressed person's behavior. But you'll find it easier to express that anger clearly and appropriately if you don't take the person's actions personally.

- **Take care of your own needs too** Make sure that whatever is going on in your relationship is something you can handle. If the depressed person breaks a date at the last minute because he or she "just doesn't have the energy," it's okay to express your anger and disappoint-ment. And you may decide that this is not someone with whom you can make definite plans right now. Or, if the conversation is getting boring, you may need to say some-thing like "I know you feel bad about that, but I can't hear that story again," or "I need some time to talk about myself now."

It's hard to care about someone and not have the power to make that person feel better. It's hard to watch someone suffer and not be able to help. But if you can make sure your own needs get taken care of, inside and outside the relationship, you'll be better able to offer what you *can* offer—a way to continue the relationship, to stay in contact, and to let the other person know you care.

Surviving a Loved One's Suicide

What if help comes too late and your friend or relative completes a suicide? How do you go on?

Here are some of the feelings that suicide survivors commonly experience:

- **Guilt**—"I should have done something."
- **Grief**—"How can I go on without this person?"
- **Anger**—"How could they leave me like this?"
- **Fear**—"They couldn't make it; what if I can't either?"
- **Helplessness**—"Someone I loved needed me, but I just couldn't do anything."
- **Shame**—"I must not be a very good person if I couldn't help someone I loved—and now everyone knows it."
- **Disgust**—"I can't believe they could do something so awful—how could they?"
- **Rejection**—"I cared about them so much, but I guess they couldn't be bothered to stay alive for me."
- **Relief**—"They've been so unhappy for so long. At least I don't have to worry about them any more."

All of these feelings are natural, and most people feel all of them at one time or another. Perhaps one will dominate at first, to be replaced by another in a few weeks or months. Or perhaps you will feel them all at once. Or, when you first hear the news, you may feel numb—in shock—until finally the feelings hit.

We'd like to offer the same advice to you that we've offered to people who consider suicide—*get help.* You've been through a terribly difficult experience, and you don't have to continue on alone. Find people to talk to who will let you explore your feelings without judging or criticizing— a sympathetic friend, a support group of other "suicide survivors," a therapist or counselor. Surviving the death of any loved one is painful enough; surviving a suicide is especially painful, and there's no reason not to mobilize all the resources you can to help you.

Suicide and the Community

So far we've talked about individual ways of coping with suicidal feelings and actions. But the community also has a role to play in suicide. As we saw in Chapter 1 in our discussion of cluster suicides, rootless communities in which people remain isolated from one another help to foster suicide. We might say that suicide is the symptom that shows just how deadly isolation and the loss of community can be.

If suicide seems to be a problem at your school, perhaps you can all do something about it together. Organize a school assembly on the topic, or put together discussion groups or support groups. Maybe you could organize a school "speak out," in which students speak out to share their experiences and thoughts about this painful issue. You might help establish a suicide hot line in your community, or go to volunteer at one that already exists. Many areas have teen suicide hot lines staffed by teenagers themselves. Can you think of other kinds of collective action you might take? You may find that the very experience of thinking about the problem together and working in a group to solve it helps to ease the sense of isolation and helplessness that makes suicide seem like the only way out.

Choosing Life

When a teenager attempts or commits suicide, what does that person really want? At first glance, we might say the person wants to die. But that may not be true—particularly for the person whose attempt is not completed. Even the teenager whose suicide is completed may not really want death but, rather, a different kind of life.

"When young people are suicidal, they're not necessarily thinking about death being preferable, they're thinking about life being intolerable," says Sally Casper, former director of a suicide prevention agency in Lawrence, Massachusetts. "They're not thinking of where they're going, they're thinking of what they're escaping from."

A girl quoted by George Howe Colt in *The Enigma of Suicide* reinforces this idea. "I want to kill myself, but I don't want to be dead," she says. "I mean, I want to be dead but I don't want to be dead forever, I only want to be dead until my 18 birthday."

"I thought death would be the happiest place to be," said a 17-year-old Texas girl who attempted suicide three times after breaking up with her boyfriend. As quoted in *Newsweek*, she said, "I thought it would be like freedom, instantly. You'd be flying around happy and you wouldn't be tied down to earth."

An adult woman remembering her two teenage attempts at suicide agrees that she didn't really want to die. Instead, she says, "I wanted to show my family death to bring life into the family." As a teenager, this woman felt that her family could deal with her image only, with her outward appearance as a nice, happy girl. By dramatizing her pain and her intense unhappiness with the way things were, this girl hoped that her family would start to deal with her in a new way, a "lively" authentic way. She now realizes that people who commit or attempt suicide really want "the things that *life* can give you. Not death. You don't know death!"

Part of what suicidal teenagers want is for the pain simply to stop. "If I died, I wouldn't hurt as much as I do now," said one 14-year-old girl to psychologist Alan Berman. Psychologists who deal with suicidal teenagers want to tell their distressed patients, "I can get you away from the pain *without* dying." The problem is, when someone is in pain, that may be a hard message to hear—and an even harder message to believe.

Until very recently, suicide was considered the ultimate taboo. It was not a subject that could be discussed openly; rather, it was the occasion for fear and superstition. Early societies feared that the suicide's ghost might return, wanting revenge against the people who had somehow driven him or her to self-murder. To protect themselves against these vengeful ghosts, they buried suicides at crossroads, hoping that the extra traffic there would keep the spirits from rising, thinking that even if a ghost or two *did* make its way aboveground, it might be confused by the crossroads and be unable to find its way home. Christian societies continued the custom, thinking that the cross in the roads would help disperse the evil.

Later philosophers and psychologists suggested that this fear of suicide is the terror that comes from guilt. Somehow, they say, we know we have failed a person driven to self-murder, and so we fear that person's revenge.

Even today, the notion of suicide brings up anger, fear, and guilt. As recently as 50 years ago, societies actually gave out legal punishments to those who attempted suicide. And doctors in today's emergency rooms often get angry with those who have attempted to kill themselves. "Why don't you just take a knife and make a real good, deep cut?" said one emergency room worker to a suicidal patient. A teenage girl reported that her doctor promised to sew her up "so I could see the scar always."

Yet despite the powerful feelings that surround the subject, suicide is no longer the taboo that it once was. Now countless articles, studies, made-for-TV movies, and instructional videotapes deal with the topic. Many states have mandated suicide prevention programs in their schools; many teenagers have openly discussed the topic in class. News reports of "cluster" suicides made suicide a popular nationwide topic.

A. Alvarez, author of *The Savage God* and himself an attempted suicide, sees the value of open discussion. But he also notes that, in taking the taboo away from suicide, we may also have muted our sense of horror. No one attempts or completes suicide unless something is terribly wrong in that person's life; suicide, whether attempted or completed, comes out of a terrible passion to do away with pain, to connect to one's true feelings, to make one's life have meaning.

The tragedy, as Alvarez says, is that it can never accomplish those goals. As he writes about his own suicide attempt:

I thought death would be like that: a synoptic vision of life, crisis by crisis, all suddenly explained, justified, redeemed, a Last Judgement in the coils and circuits of the brain. Instead, all I got was a hole in the head, a round zero, nothing. I'd been swindled.

Months after he had recovered, Alvarez writes, he finally accepted that he could not really "explain" his life:

Once I had accepted that there weren't ever going to be any answers, even in death, I found to my surprise that I didn't much care whether I was happy or unhappy; "problems" and "the problems of problems" no longer existed. And that in itself is already the beginning of happiness.

Although suicide, death, and life may remain mysterious, that doesn't prevent us from making choices about what to choose and how to live. Finding or making the meaning in your life, facing your pain and transforming it into something useful, making the changes in your life that you need to go on—these are the great challenges of growing up, of being alive, of being human. Although the difficulties may seem overwhelming at times, the rewards, when they come, can also overwhelm us with relief, with satisfaction, with joy. Elsewhere in his book, Alvarez quotes the philosopher Albert Camus, who called life a gift that is absurd, but real. "In other words," says Alvarez, "the final argument against suicide is life itself."

6

Where to Find Help

Suicide

The American Association of Suicidology (AAS) compiled this list from a variety of sources and does not guarantee the accuracy, reliability, or completeness of this information. Neither the AAS nor the authors of this book have undertaken any independent review or examination of the organizations listed. Both the AAS and the authors specifically disclaim any liability or responsibility for any actions or statements by any of the organizations listed. All information and statements contained in this directory are provided by and the responsibility of the organizations who have provided the information or statements to AAS. Publication of this list does not imply any opinion, endorsement, or approval of the AAS, its officers or members, or by the authors or publishers of this book. The listing is offered for information only.

Many of the organizations listed serve the friends and families of suicide victims or can provide referrals to suicide survivor self-help groups. They also include resources for those coping with drug and alcohol abuse, and eating disorders.

Alabama

Contact Mobile
P.O. Box 66608
Mobile, AL 36660
crisis phone: 334-431-5111
business phone: 334-431-5100
available 24 hours a day

Crisis Center, Inc.
3600 8th Avenue South
Suite 501
Birmingham, AL 35222
crisis phone: 205-323-7777
business phone: 205-323-7782
available 24 hours a day

Arizona

Help On Call Crisis Line
P.O. Box 43696
Tucson, AZ 85733
crisis phone: 520-323-9373
business phone: 520-881-8045
available 24 hours a day

Terros Behavioral Health Services
320 East Virginia Avenue
Phoenix, AZ 85004
602-266-1100

Arkansas

Northwest Arkansas Crisis Intervention Center
P.O. Box 1618
Springdale, AR 72765
crisis phone: 501-756-2337
            888-CRISIS-2
business phone: 501-756-1995
available 24 hours a day

California

Suicide Prevention Center
crisis phone: 310-391-1253
available 24 hours a day

Crisis Support Services of Alameda County
P.O. Box 9102
Berkeley, CA 94709
crisis phone: 510-849-2212 Oakland, Berkeley
            510-889-1333 Hayward, Castro Valley
            510-794-5211 Fremont, Union City
            510-449-5566 Livermore Valley area
business phone: 510-848-1515
available 24 hours a day

Teen Line
Thalians Mental Health Center
P.O. Box 48750
Los Angeles, CA 90048
statewide toll free: 800-852-8336
crisis phone: 310-855-4673
business phone: 310-855-3401
staffed 6:00 P.M. to 10:00 P.M.

Colorado

Suicide and Crisis Hot Line
Capitol Hill Community Center, Box 15
1290 Williams
Denver, CO 80218
crisis phone: 303-860-1200
available 24 hours a day

Connecticut

The Samaritans, Inc. of the Capital Region
P.O. Box 12004
Hartford, CT 06112
crisis phone: 860-232-2121
business phone: 860-232-9559

Delaware

Contact Delaware, Inc.
P.O. Box 9525
Wilmington, DE 19809
crisis phone: 302-761-9100
TTY: 302-761-9700
in Delaware: 800-262-9800
business phone: 302-761-9800
available 24 hours a day

District of Columbia

D.C. Hotline, Inc.
P.O. Box 57194
Washington, DC 20037
crisis phone: 202-223-2255
business phone: 202-223-0020
available 24 hours a day

Florida

Switchboard of Miami, Inc.
444 Prickell Avenue, Suite 450
Miami, FL 33131
crisis phone: 305-358-4357
The Link (youth hotline): 305-377-8336
business phone: 305-358-1640
available 24 hours a day

Georgia

Emergency Mental Health Service
Fulton County Division of Mental Health
132 Mitchell Street
Atlanta, GA 30303
crisis phone: 404-730-1600
TTY: 404-730-1608
business phone: 404-730-1600
available 24 hours a day

Hawaii

Helping Hands Hawaii
680 Iwilei Road
#430
Honolulu, HI 96817
suicide and Crisis Center: 808-521-4555
crisis phone: 808-521-4556
business phone: 808-536-7234
available 24 hours a day

Idaho

Emergency Line
Region IV Service/Mental Health Center
1720 Westgate Drive
Boise, ID 83704
crisis phone: 208-334-0808

business phone: 208-334-0800
available 24 hours a day

Illinois

Affiliated Psychologist Ltd.
4801 West Peterson
Suite 525
Chicago, IL 60646
crisis phone: 773-286-3100
business phone: 773-286-3100
available 24 hours a day

Indiana

Mental Health Association in Marion County
Crisis and Suicide Intervention Service
2506 Willowbrook Parkway
#100
Indianapolis, IN 46205-1542
crisis phone: 317-251-7575
business phone: 317-251-0005
available 24 hours a day

Iowa

Community Telephone Service Crisis Line
Service of the American Red Cross
2116 Grand Avenue
Des Moines, IA 50312
crisis phone: 515-244-1000
counseling: 515-244-1010
AIDS hotline statewide: 800-445-2437
business phone: 515-244-6700
available Monday–Friday 3:00 P.M. to 8:00 A.M.
Saturday, Sunday and holidays 24 hours

Kansas
Wyandot Mental Health
3615 Eaton Avenue
Kansas City, KS 66103
crisis phone: 913-831-1773
business phone: 913-831-9500
available 24 hours a day

Kentucky
The Crisis and Information Center
101 West Muhammad Ali Boulevard
Louisville, KY 40202-1429
crisis phone: 502-589-4313
TDD: 502-589-4259
Kentucky WATTS line: 800-221-0446
FAX: 502-589-8756
business phone: 502-589-8630
available 24 hours a day

Louisiana
Volunteer and Information Agency
4747 Earhart Boulevard
Suite 200
New Orleans, LA 70125
crisis phone: 504-523-2673
business phone: 504-488-4636
available 24 hours a day

Maine
Crisis Stabilization Unit
P.O. Box 588
Skowhegan, ME 04976
crisis phone: 207-474-2506
Skowhegan (dispatcher): 800-357-4343
children's services only: 800-400-2506
business phone: 207-474-2564
available 24 hours a day

Maryland

First Step Youth Services Center
8303 Liberty Road
Baltimore, MD 21244
crisis phone: 410-521-3800
business phone: 410-521-4141
available Monday to Thursday 9:00 A.M.–9:00 P.M.;
Friday 9:00 A.M.–5:00 P.M.; Saturday 9:00 A.M.–1:00 P.M.

Massachusetts

The Samaritans
500 Commonwealth Avenue
Boston, MA 02215
crisis phone: 617-247-0220
Samariteen Line, 2 P.M. to 11 P.M. daily: 617-247-8050
toll free, MA & NH only: 800-252-8336
business phone: 617-536-2460
available 24 hours a day

Michigan

NSO Emergency Telephone Service/
  Suicide Prevention Center
220 Bagley
Suite 840
Detroit, MI 48226
crisis phone: 313-224-7000
business phone: 313-961-1060
available 24 hours a day

Minnesota

Crisis Intervention Center
Hennepin County Medical Center
701 Park Avenue South
Minneapolis, MN 55415
crisis phone: 612-347-3161
suicide line: 612-347-2222

sexual assault line: 612-347-5832
Behavioral Emergency Outreach: 612-347-2011
business phone: 612-347-3164
available 24 hours a day

Mississippi

Contact Helpline
P.O. Box 1304
Columbus, MS 39703-1304
crisis phone: 601-328-0200
            601-327-4357
business phone: 601-327-2968
available 24 hours a day

Missouri

Life Crisis Services, Inc.
1423 South Big Bend Boulevard
St. Louis, MO 63117
crisis phone: 314-647-4357
business phone: 314-647-3100
available 24 hours a day

Montana

Department of Public Health and Human Sevices
Children and Family Services Division
2508 3rd Avenue North
Billings, MT 59101
crisis phone: 406-657-3120
            406-255-6930
business phone: 406-657-3120
available 24 hours a day

Nebraska

Father Flanagan's Boys Home
Boys Town National Hotline

Town Hall
Boys Town, NE 68010
national hotline: 800-448-3000
national hotline TDD: 800-448-1833
available 24 hours a day

Nevada

Suicide Prevention Center of Clark County
3838 Raymert
Las Vegas, NV 89121
crisis phone: 702-731-2990
business phone: 702-731-2990
available 24 hours a day

New Hampshire

Mental Health Center of Greater Manchester
401 Cypress Street
Manchester, NH 03103
603-668-4111
available 24 hours a day

New Jersey

Emergency Psychiatric Services
100 Bergen Street
Newark, NJ 07103
crisis phone: 201-623-2323
business phone: 201-972-0480
available 24 hours a day

New Mexico

University of New Mexico Mental Health Center
2600 Marble Northeast
Albuquerque, NM 87131
general clinic: 505-272-2174
crisis phone: 505-247-1121
available 24 hours a day

New York

The Samaritans of New York
P.O. Box 1259
Madison Square Station
New York, NY 10159
crisis phone: 212-673-3000
available 24 hours a day

North Dakota

Help-Line
c/o Mental Health Association of North Dakota
P.O. Box 160
Bismarck, ND 58502
crisis phone: 800-472-2911
business phone: 701-255-3692
available 24 hours a day

Ohio

Columbia St. Vincent Charity Hospital
Psychiatric Emergency Service
2351 East 22nd Street
Cleveland, OH 44115
crisis phone: 216-623-6888
business phone: 216-861-6200
available 24 hours a day

Oklahoma

Teenline, Oklahoma City
Department of Mental Health
P.O. Box 53277
Oklahoma City, OK 73152-3277
teenline local: 405-271-8336
teenline toll free: 800-522-8336, 800-522-8398
business phone: 405-522-3908
available noon–midnight

Oregon
Metro Crisis Intervention Service
P.O. Box 637
Portland, OR 97207
crisis phone: 503-223-6161
business phone: 503-226-3099
available 24 hours a day

Pennsylvania
Philadelphia Suicide and Crisis Center
1 Reading Center
1101 Market, 7th Floor
Philadelphia, PA 19107
crisis phone: 215-686-4420
business phone: 215-686-4420
available 24 hours a day

Rhode Island
The Samaritans of Rhode Island's Suicide Prevention and
  Education Center
2 Magee Street
Providence, RI 02906
crisis phone: 401-272-4044
Rhode Island only: 800-365-4044
business phone: 401-272-4243
available 24 hours a day

South Carolina
Hotline, Inc.
P.O. Box 71583
North Charleston, SC 29415-1583
crisis phone: 803-744-4357
statewide: 800-922-2283
teen line 4:00 to 8:00 P.M. Monday–Friday: 803-747-8336
teen line 4:00 to 8:00 P.M. Monday–Friday: 800-273-8225

business phone: 803-747-3007
available 24 hours a day

South Dakota
Crisis Line, Volunteer and Information Center
Family Services
1000 Northwest Avenue, Suite 310
Sioux Falls, SD 57104-1314
crisis phone: 605-339-4357
business phone: 605-334-6646
available 24 hours a day

Tennessee
Charter Lakeside Hospital
2911 Brunswick Road
Memphis, TN 38133
crisis phone: 901-377-4733
crisis phone for states bordering Tennessee: 800-232-5253
business phone: 901-377-4700
available 24 hours a day

Texas
Contact Counseling and Crisis Line
P.O. Box 800742
Dallas, TX 75380-0742
crisis phone: 972-233-2233
teen hot line: 972-233-8336
business phone: 972-233-0866
available 24 hours a day

Crisis Intervention of Houston, Inc.
P.O. Box 130866
Houston, TX 77219
crisis hot line Central: 713-228-1505
crisis hot line Bay Area: 281-461-9992
Spanish hot line: 713-526-8088
teenline: 713-529-8336

business phone: 713-527-9864
available 24 hours a day

Vermont
Hotline For Help, Inc.
4 High Street, Suite 6
Brattleboro, VT 05301
crisis phone: 802-257-7989
business phone: 802-257-7980
available 9:00 A.M.–10:00 P.M. Monday–Friday

Washington
Crisis Clinic of King County
1515 Dexter Avenue North
#300
Seattle, WA 98109
crisis phone: 206-461-3222
business phone: 206-461-3210
available 24 hours a day

Wisconsin
Helpline
P.O. Box 92455
Milwaukee, WI 53202
crisis phone: 414-271-3123
TDD: 414-271-6039
business phone: 414-276-8487
available 24 hours a day

Wyoming
Cheyenne Helpline
307-634-4469
available 24 hours a day

Canada

Canadian Mental Health Association, Suicide Services
723 14th St. NW, #103
Calgary, AB T2N 2A4
crisis phone: 403-297-1744 available 9:00 A.M.–5:00 P.M.
403-266-1605 available 24 hours a day
business phone: 403-297-1700

Centre de Prevention du Suicide (CPS)
Quebec, PQ
crisis line: 418-683-4588
business phone: 418-683-0933
available 24 hours a day

Crisis Intervention and Suicide Prevention Center for
  Greater Vancouver
763 East Broadway
Vancouver, BC V5T 1X8
crisis phone: 604-872-3311
business phone: 604-872-1811
available 24 hours a day

Distress Centre of Ottawa
P. O. Box 70039
160 Elgin Street, Main Plaza
Ottawa, ON K2P 2M3
crisis phone: 613-238-3311 available 24 hours a day
youthline (peer staffed 4 P.M. to 11 P.M.): 613-238-2088
business phone: 613-238-1089

Toronto East General Hospital
Department of Psychiatry
825 Coxwell Avenue
Toronto, ON M4C 3E7
business phone: 416-461-8272
crisis phone: 416-469-6220
available 9:00 A.M.–5:00 P.M. Monday–Friday

Saskatoon Crisis Intervention Service
1410 20th Street West
Saskatoon, SK S7M 0Z4
306-933-6200
available 24 hours a day

Additional Resources

The following organizations can provide you with referrals and advice in dealing with problems that may be related to teenage suicide.

Alcohol and Drug Problems

Al-Anon Family Group Headquarters
200 Park Avenue South, Room 814
New York, NY 10003
212-254-7230
212-260-0407
See the white pages for the group in your area. Al-Anon helps those over the age of 8 deal with problems created by alcoholism in friends or family members.

Alcoholics Anonymous World Services
475 Riverside Drive
New York, NY 10115
212-870-3400
Provides free referrals for those seeking recovery from alcohol problems.

Eating Disorders

Anorexia Nervosa and Related Eating Disorders, Inc. (ANRED)
P.O. Box 5102
Eugene, OR 97405
541-344-1144

Eating Disorder Program
Ward 7A
Toronto Hospital for Sick Children
555 University Avenue
Toronto, Ontario
Canada M5G 1X8
416-813-7195

Eating Disorders Program
B.C.'s Children's Hospital
4480 Oak Street
Vancouver, British Columbia
Canada V6H 3V4
604-875-2200

Physical and Sexual Abuse

Children's Aid Society
33 Charles Street East
Toronto, Ontario
Canada M4Y 1R9
416-924-4646

Kempe National Center for the Prevention and Treatment
   of Child Abuse and Neglect
1205 Oneida Street
Denver, CO 80220-2944
303-321-3963

National Clearinghouse on Child Abuse and
   Neglect Information
   (a divison of The National Center on Child Abuse and
   Neglect/Children's Bureau—NCCAN)
P.O. Box 1182
Washington, DC 20013-1182
800-394-3366
703-385-7565

For Further Reading

The following books will provide further information on teenage suicide.

Alvarez, A. *The Savage God*. New York: W.W. Norton, 1990.

Colt, George Howe. *The Enigma of Suicide*. New York: Simon & Schuster, 1991.

Dolce, Laura. *Suicide*. New York: Chelsea House Publishers, 1991.

Flanders, Stephen. *Suicide*. New York: Facts On File, 1991.

Francis, Dorothy R. *Suicide: A Preventable Tragedy*. New York: E.P. Dutton, 1987.

Gardner, Sandra. *Teenage Suicide*. New York: Simon & Schuster, 1991.

Hyde, Margaret O. and Elizabeth H. Forsyth, *Suicide*. New York: Franklin Watts Publishers, 1991.

Leder, Jane M. *Dead Serious: A Book for Teenagers about Teenage Suicide*. New York: Avon Books, 1989.

McGuire, Leslie. *Suicide* (Troubled Society Series). Vero Beach, FL: Rourke Corporation, 1990.

Miller, Michael. *Dare to Live: A Guide to the Prevention and Understanding of Teenage Suicide*. Hillsboro, OR: Beyond Words Publishing, 1989.

Powell, Donnalynn. *A Reason to Live*. Minneapolis, MN: Bethany House Publishers, 1989.

Schliefer, Jay. *Everything You Need to Know about Teen Suicide*. New York: Rosen Publishing, 1990.

INDEX

0285303069